RECYCLING A SON OF THE BRITISH RAJ

Dear Gordon

Glad to work with you
on IHM issues.
Thank you for your support.

Peter 9/14/15

RECYCLING A SON OF THE BRITISH RAJ

Peter Ramrayka

First published by Hansib Publications in 2015

Hansib Publications Limited
P.O. Box 226, Hertford, Hertfordshire, SG14 3WY
United Kingdom
info@hansibpublications.com

www.hansibpublications.com

RAF Crests reproduced on pages 77, 81, 82, 83, 89, 90, 99,
by kind permission M.O.D.

ISBN 978-1-910553-24-4

A CIP catalogue record for this book
is available from the British Library

Production
Hansib Publications Limited

Printed in Great Britain

Contents

PREFACE

Your beliefs become your thoughts. Your thoughts become your words. Your words become your actions. Your actions become your habits. Your habits become your values. Your values become your destiny.

Mahatma Gandhi

The year is 1961. As a 17-year-old Indian-Guyanese boy I would leave the comfort of my tropical paradise multi-racial, multi-religious home, and head for the streets of London which I thought were paved with gold!

Imbued with a sense of excited anticipation and harbouring ambitions of becoming a lawyer, as an observant teenager I soon found out that they were NOT as I settled into bed-sit accommodation and embarked on a journey of discovery that would take me around the world.

Back in British Guiana, my place of birth, I had been told that 'Mother England' was inhabited by decent, fair minded and friendly people who would welcome me and my colonial brothers with open arms. The British Empire wouldn't have been the greatest in the world without us – would it?

But over a period of more than half a century I would discover that issues of colour, race, religion, and culture were as divisive as they were cohesive. But in a twist of fate that led me to the top of my chosen profession, I somehow managed to escape the clutches of overt discrimination.

First career stop was the Royal Air Force where I spent nine years rising up the ranks of the medical administration branch. Just as I was considering applying to become an officer I switched sectors and joined the National Health Service. It was during this time that I led or became involved in many of the major re-organisational changes in the NHS (becoming the first person of Asian descent to be appointed to a Chief Administrator's post in a District Health Authority) including the run down and closing of the first and one of the largest Learning Disability Hospitals in England and moving patients into the community. I embraced British systems and techniques and started to promote them internationally.

I then became a healthcare management consultant and worked on many exciting and innovative projects abroad. Highlights included managing the building of new healthcare facilities to transform a small hospital into a National Referral Hospital in Botswana, strengthening healthcare structure and clinical services in Pakistan and being in charge of a flying teaching eye hospital which travelled to third world countries helping restore people's sight.

Returning to the NHS, firstly in Scotland to run down and close the last of the major Learning Disability Hospitals in that country (again moving the patients into local communities) and then to London to lead the building of two multi-million pounds national and international award winning state of the art facilities for mental health patients.

My life in public service extended to other areas - in particular politics, the magistracy and voluntary services in the UK and Tanzania. I regularly rubbed shoulders with the rich, the famous, the movers and shakers in society – including Royalty!

In *Recycling a Son of the British Raj*, I looked back on my life and assessed whether, as Gandhiji suggested, my values determined my destiny. I concluded, amongst other things, that major aspects of my life had been influenced by my affiliation and admiration of India – the spiritual home of my forefathers and the glorious civilisation that I was (and am) so proud to be a part of.

INTRODUCTION

These memoirs were started at the suggestion of various family members and friends who thought that my diversified professional and voluntary experiences of various aspects of life would be of direct interest to them (especially those scattered around the world) and a wide range of people I had been in contact with. It was also felt that, as I my roots were in British Guiana, a country to which the British Raj in India had systematically and controversially exported indentured labourers in the mid-19th century (after slavery was abolished) my voluntary journey as a teenager to the United Kingdom (in particular England), acquisition of British culture and values and my subsequent promotion of those values to the sub – continent of my ancestors in India, Pakistan, and elsewhere where the British flag once flew, would be an excellent example of recycling and would also appeal to a wider readership.

The challenges that I had were many! I needed to record the experiences of my early life in British Guiana (and I have generally used this spelling in the first part of the book for authenticity changing over to the 1966 post independent spelling Guyana, now used by the country) as these were intertwined with my close family many of whom are named as they were direct descendants of indentured labourers from India. That they retained their culture and customs in a foreign environment and prospered in the country of their adoption were noteworthy achievements. A balance had to be struck between giving the reader brief background contextual information without turning the book into a full historical tome. There are many other academic and historical books in which these aspects are comprehensively covered.

The second challenge was that as the focus of the book was on my professional and voluntary work it was suggested that I should limit detailed references to my immediate family life, only recording those incidents which were directly relevant to a particular event or occurrence. Needless to say that my wife, Rookmini, and my two daughters, Nadia and Tara, were of direct support and comfort to me throughout my professional life and I acknowledge with gratitude their contributions to my achievements.

In my work I had met and interacted with a considerable number of people in all walks of life from Presidents and Prime Ministers to raw recruits from the Royal Air Force. All have, in various ways, influenced my views and some have helped to shape my life. I have named some of them and for those who are currently living and I felt might be shy of publicity I have given pseudonyms. I have no doubt that they would recognise themselves! Again, I record my appreciation and thanks for their contribution through various stages of my working life.

The third challenge was that the book was being written for different audiences (some would have detailed knowledge of events described, others less so) as my disparate career span early life in Guiana, the Royal Air Force, the National Health Service, overseas health management consultancies (both paid and voluntary), voluntary work and my involvement in politics. I had, therefore, to provide sufficient information to make incidents understandable to a variety of readers without delving too deeply into particular areas. I have a companion (I will introduce him later!) a 'critical friend' who will let me know when a particular technical or unfamiliar issue needs further explaining.

Also as I have had, from time to time, to use non-English words (Dutch, Hindi and Urdu) in describing foreign places, events and things. I have wherever possible put English translation in parenthesis after or before these words.

The final and perhaps the most significant challenge was to be honest about my experiences as someone who had spent the majority of my life in a country other than my place of birth. There is always an indigenous sensitivity about comments which can be interpreted as criticising one's adopted country. This can be so, even though I have been fully integrated into its culture and values and have demonstrated my passionate loyalty credentials. I hope that I have met that challenge by sharing my views, controversial as some might be (especially on cultural and race relations issues) without rancour as I felt to do otherwise would lack integrity and would be dishonest to readers.

When I left British Guiana in 1961 as a young boy, apart from wanting to travel explore and develop educationally, I did not, and do not, subscribe to the view that my **Fate (Kismat)** was predetermined by the course of events. I believed that - **Fortitude (Dhariya)** - resilience, strength of mind and character would enable me to endure diversity with courage and so it has turned out. **Fortune (Bhagya)** – came not by winning the lottery but by a series of events and opportunities which have led to favourable outcomes.

My memoirs are a small contribution to the development of the multi - cultural fabric of British society. I have expressed, in my own way, events which I felt are relevant to share and have given glimpses of what it was like in moving from one society to another and the satisfaction it had given me to come through the mill smiling!

My wife Rookmini, daughters Nadia (left) and Tara (right)

PROLOGUE

In Guianese mythology invisible little beings called *BACOOS*, come from the spirit world (similar to the Irish leprechaun) and can live in various places in a house including in bottles. They are known to reward their owners with untold wealth and good fortune once fed with bananas and milk. However, like a poltergeist they can create mayhem by moving things around, throwing stones and causing general commotion if provoked. Under certain conditions, especially if felt threatened Bacoos can (and do) make themselves visible. Bacoos in my country of birth, British Guiana, speak to their companions in patois English. Their conversations can only be heard by the two of them.

In June 1961, I was sitting having lunch on a bench in Main Street, a tree lined avenue in Georgetown, the capital, when I saw what I thought was an empty rum bottle, with the top securely on, rolling from side to side. As there was no wind or other reason for the bottle to be moving I thought this rather strange and took a closer look. What I saw was an embryonic being gesticulating with its hands for me to open the bottle and let it out. With some trepidation I did just that and out popped a tiny male doll like figure, smelling of rum and swaying from side. Its first words were: *"Tank yo massah, me lil groggy cos me previous owna push me in the rum bottle without washing it and fumes woz making me giddy. Me name Basdeo, and me know dat you name Peter and you ah plan to go live on an island across the Atlantic called Hengland (sic)."*

Astonished by this I questioned Basdeo;

"How do you know my name and my plans to go to England?"

Basdeo replied *"Me can see in the future, but not in the past, me met yo Aajee,yo fadder mudder* (paternal grandmother) *and she say what you is about to do remind she when she first arrive in Demerara from India in 1904 because she woz 18 and you ah a lil pickney* (little child) *at 17!"*

15

Suspicious, but intrigued, I asked Basdeo what he asked of me and he replied that he wanted us to be friends. He also requested that I put him back in a clean bottle, feed him well with bananas and milk and he would be by my side to help as I reflect on my life's journey. I pondered on this for a while and said to him:

"Let's make a deal if you are a good Bacoo, watch over me but don't interfere and try to speak PROPER English, then I will do all that you ask".

Basdeo hesitated for a moment, scratched his head and replied:

"We got da deal but forgive me if me can't speak dis way all the time because it will be hard. Thank you Massa". He added: "And instead of calling you Massa, which is a term used by slaves, who were brought from West Africa to work on the sugar plantation I call you Mr. Peter, Peter Ji or Peter Sahib which I know are terms used by your Indian forefathers when addressing people they respect. Also I will ask you some personal questions about yourself, and explanations from time to time, which will help me and others to understand the background, put into context some of the challenges you have experienced and the difference you have made in your life's journey".

I replied:

"Yes Basdeo, you can call me Peter Sahib that will be splendid. Now, what is you first question?"

Basdeo grinned and said:

"Tell me lil bit, sorry a little bit about British Guiana".

So I did...and this is what I told him.

CHAPTER 1

CULTURAL TRANSPLANTATION
BIHAR TO DEMERARA

HOME – BRITISH GUIANA – A BRIEF HISTORY

In the fifteenth century, the country we now know as Guyana was considered to be in the region of Sir Walter Raleigh's mythical El Dorado (although the actual place was thought to be in present day Venezuela). Raleigh led people from Europe and in particular England to believe that there was a wonderful rich land where gold was plentiful just waiting to be inhabited. This encouraged European adventurers to compete to find this revered place and not surprisingly the major European powers of the day kept fighting each other for supremacy in the area which to them was part of what they called the 'New World' (although the indigenous people called Amerindians had lived there for many centuries).

"Peter Sahib, why are they called Amerindians?"

"Well Basdeo there was an Italian sailor called Christopher Columbus who wanted to find a sea passage to India but the French and English royalty at the time would not support him. In desperation, he sought the assistance of the King and Queen of Spain, Ferdinand and Isabella who agreed to sponsor him. He and a crew of three ships set sail in August 1492 to cross the Atlantic Ocean and ten weeks later they landed in a place we now call the Bahamas. Columbus saw the indigenous brown people, who had been living there for centuries and thinking he had stumbled across India called the people 'Indios' Spanish for Indians hence present day Amerindians".

"Thanks Peter Sahib, so this man Columbus set out not knowing where he was going, ended up not knowing where he was and did it all on borrowed money from the King and Queen of Spain?"

"Yes, it's quite amusing, don't you think? But one other thing Basdeo, Columbus was not the first European to reach the so called New World. There was a Norse expedition in the 11th Century headed by a chap called Leif Ericson but his adventures have been glossed over in some history books particularly those giving a partisan view of their concepts of civilisation and the world's development. These, however, need to be taken with a large pinch of salt as I will explain from time to time as we go along.

Now returning to the development of British Guiana, after the lunacy of Raleigh, Essequibo, which became the first of its counties, was occupied by the Dutch in 1596 at a place called Nova Zeelandia (New Zeeland). By 1613 Kyk-over-al (See over All) was established and this led to the colonisation of another place, called Berbice in 1627. It subsequently became a second county.

Competition in Europe for foreign conquests by French, Dutch and English nations spilled over into Essequibo and Berbice and during this period swamp lands were drained and brought into use for sugar, coffee and cotton cultivation making the area attractive and profitable to Europeans. A Dutch Commander of Essequibo, Laurens Storm Van Gravesande, expanded into another area, called Demerara (which became Guiana's third county) and encouraged people, would be entrepreneurs from Spain, Germany, France, Sweden and Denmark to settle. By 1781 the British had captured Essequibo, Demerara and Berbice but the French and Dutch did not give up the fight easily and the lands changed hands relatively frequently, finally being ceded to the British in 1814 by the Treaty of Paris. The colony of British Guiana came into being in 1831 with the former Dutch capital, Stabroek in Demerara being renamed Georgetown, after the British King George III. That is the reason, Basdeo, why there are so many Dutch names and influences in the country–I already mentioned Nova Zeelandia and Kyk-over-al, others with their English meanings include Ruimveld (spacious field) in Georgetown, De Kendren (the children) on the East Coast of Guiana and at various places across the length and breadth of the country. There were also Dutch legacies such as elaborate systems for draining the land using dykes and kokers!"

"Boy, sorry I mean Peter Sahib, Guiana really has a fascinating development history, hasn't it".

"Yes Basdeo, from a barren coast land flooded by the sea to one of the most agricultural productive areas in the region. It became known as the Caribbean bread basket; so described because Guiana was five times larger than all the other English speaking Caribbean territories put together and had much spare land to produce rice and sugar"

"Thanks Peter Sahib, but who was responsible for developing this area and making it fertile?"

"Well, Basdeo, this is a long story but I will condense it. During the time that European nations were fighting over the area their countrymen, who had become 'land owners' were encouraging their own kith and kin (in particular those from Holland, England, Scotland, Portugal and Malta) to join them. But these people proved not to be strong or resilient enough to withstand the harsh climatic challenges and do all the very hard work required to develop the land so the 'land owners' started recruiting workers from further afield – specifically Africa and Asia.

With the cooperation of tribal leaders, they enticed or kidnapped people from Africa, treated them as sub human beings, called them slaves and transported them in appalling conditions across the seas from Africa to British Guiana, with many dying on the way. Then, once those who had survived had landed, they were put to work in terrible conditions on plantations to produce sugar and other agricultural products for export to the European markets.

ABOLITION OF SLAVERY AND START OF INDENTURED LABOURERS FROM INDIA

In 1838 the Europeans changed moral directions and decided to abolish slavery. Many of the freed slaves refused to continue working on the plantations and the Europeans, by then mostly British and Dutch looked around the world for people in lands they had 'conquered' or entered into protectionist agreement with (in particular the Maharajahs (Kings) Rajahs and Nawabs (Princes) of Hindu and Muslim principalities in the ancient lands of India). There then followed massive emigration to British Guiana from the Indian sub-continent then under the British Raj (rule). The immigration of relatively large numbers of Indians from 1838, to replace the freed slaves, proved to be extremely successful in developing the agricultural sector in the colony, in particular the sugar plantations. But it also sowed the seeds of distrust and enmity between Africans and Indians - a situation which unfortunately still lingers amongst some of their respective descendants. The crux of the problem was that Africans saw Indians diluting their ability to force the mainly British plantation owners to pay them properly and to treat them with dignity and respect"

"So, Peter Sahib, was this how your forefathers came to be transported from India to British Guiana?"

"Yes, Basdeo, and to identify them separately from the indigenous people whom Columbus had foolishly called 'Indios' or Amerindians these people were called 'East ' Indians. But first let me give you a brief background of the British Raj then I will answer your question".

INDO- GUIANESE AND THE BRITISH RAJ

"In Guiana we were taught that British citizens went around the world initially developing trade links and transforming some of those areas into crown possessions and promoting Christianity. We also learnt that Britain was involved in the movement of swathes of people from one country to another as slaves, indentured labourers and in case of their own citizens, convicted for major or petty crimes, transporting them to Australia and North America as punishment.

History lessons focused on the positive effects these actions had in building up a great and modern empire, in particular India, which came under British Raj control in 1858. Disraeli, the first British Prime Minister from a Jewish background, added the trappings of an empire by proposing in 1876 that Queen Victoria should be crowned as Empress of India. This was subsequently approved by the British parliament although Victoria had never set foot in the country and many people felt that Disraeli's action was designed to 'curry favour' with the Queen with whom he had enjoyed good relations. On the Queen's death in 1901 the title passed to her son Edward V11 who became King Emperor with his Danish wife Alexandra, as Queen Empress.

History books suggest that Queen Victoria had a soft spot for India and people of Indian origin. After the death of her husband Prince Albert in 1861 and the death in 1883 of John Brown, her outdoor servant (in Scots *ghille)* with whom it is alleged she had a 'warm and loving friendship' she engaged a young Indian servant, called Abdul Karim who came to work for her in late June 1887 and very soon the pair became close (despite the 42 years age gap). Victoria started to learn Hindustani (sic) guided by Abdul, who became her Teacher (Munshi in Urdu). She would insist having an Indian dish on most of her dinner menus and on special occasions she wore the famous Koh-I-Noor (Mountain of Light) diamond.

"Peter Sahib, why is this diamond famous?"

"Basdeo, it is one of the largest in the world. In 1849 it was seized by the East India Company from the Maharajah of Lahore, as a spoil of war, and presented to Queen Victoria in 1850. It was passed down the family and ended up in the late Queen Mother's crown where it remains to this day in the Tower of London. It is the subject of a dispute and its return is being demanded by both India and Pakistan. James Callaghan, The British Prime Minister in 1976 refused the request as did one of his successors, David Cameron, when he visited India in 2013.

Queen Victoria's affection for India even extended to her filling a room at her residence, Osborne House, on the Isle of Wight with artefacts from the sub- continent. She called this her 'Durbar Room' (a place in India where indigenous Indian rulers held audience). She told people it was so that she could step into 'her own India'.

"Peter, Sahib, what do you think were the views of the of the Indian masses at the time about the Empress/Emperor titles".

"Well, Basdeo, many people knew that their 'own' Emperor, the Mughal Shah Bahadur had been banished by the British to Burma in 1837. However, Bahadur was not really Indian either! He was a foreigner from a Central Asian Mughal (Mongol) Muslim dynasty who ruled large parts of India for several hundred years. The last indigenous Hindu Emperor was Hem Chandra Vikramaditya (1501- 1556) who fought Afghans and Mughals invaders across north India, Agra and Delhi, winning scores of battles, but was eventually defeated at the Battle of Panipat. His body was desecrated by the Mughals, in a revengeful action, because he had fought so fiercely against them.

Indian masses in the villages across the country did not worry too much about distant rulers.

When the great Indian leader Mahatma Gandhi was on a tour in the state of Mysore he asked a villager who ruled Mysore (Gandhiji – the suffix 'ji' is added by Indians to the names of people to convey respect), knew that there was a Maharajah of Mysore). He had a response that some god ruled the state. Gandhiji felt that if this villager's knowledge about the ruler of his state was so perfunctory what concerns would he have of a foreign appointed Empress, especially an elderly white woman from thousands of miles away! Of course several parts of India had their own centuries old local rulers – Hindu Maharajahs and Rajahs and Muslims Nawabs who had individually reached 'agreements/ accommodation' with the British Raj to primarily safeguard their kingdoms whilst acknowledging the military supremacy of the British in areas outside of their borders. It would take 47 years for the Imperial titles to be abolished, and the restitution of total national leadership of India by Indian people although, in theory King George VI who was crowned in 1936 still had Emperor included in his many titles but finally removing it from the British crown in 1952 – five years after the Republic of India came into being. The connection continued in other forms. For example a wide range of honours associated with the period such as the Knight Grand Cross of the Star of India, Knight Commander of the Indian Empire, were proudly worn by successive royals or by others who had been given these awards."

"Peter Sahib, that was a fascinating piece of historical information but what relevance is it to Guiana?"

"Well, Basdeo, it helps us to understand the complex world of Guiana (and other similar former colonial countries) where people from different lands were used by the British to build countries which had been gifted in war, acquired through treaties of protection or as a consequence of hostile actions. These people had to develop loyalties to their new countries, learn to respect and admire the colonial power and their history while at the same time drawing strength from belonging to other cultures or civilisations. For example Indian civilisation which was centuries old (confirmed through the discovery of ancient sites at Harappa and Mohenjo Daro, now in Pakistan) judged to be on an equal historical standing with ancient Rome, Greece and Persia. That was, and still is, the challenge faced by the different races in Guiana. It has always had a particular resonance with Indo Guianese as we drew strength from being part of one of the major civilisations of the world, with centuries old customs and practices, while at the same time acknowledging that many of India's powerful attributes were over shadowed, submerged and distorted".

"Thanks Peter Sahib, continue with your family's arrival in Guiana".

Standing at Fort Kyk Over Al national monument – Constructed 1616.

Queen Victoria's statue - Law Courts - Georgetown.

Fort Kyk Over Al sign.

CHAPTER 2

ESTABLISHING NEW ROOTS
ARRIVAL AND SETTLING IN

ARRIVAL OF THE RAMREKHAS IN BRITISH GUIANA

"My own family was one of over 240,000 Indians transported from India to Guiana between 1838 and 1917 when, again, moral conscience prevailed on those involved to stop the 'trade'. In 1904 my Aajee, Salukni and my Aajhaa, RamRekha, my father's mother and father, left Calcutta on a ship called the 'Mersey' for British Guiana. My Aajee's Emigration Pass signed by the Deputy Surgeon of Depot 2525, and countersigned by the Surgeon Superintendent, the Government Emigration Agent for British Guiana and the Protector of Emigrants (a real belt and braces document!) showed that she was 18, her father's name was Bhola, from Bishunpura in Patna District, Bihar, the north Indian state where Gautama Buddha is said to have obtained Enlightenment (Bodhimandala).

The British Raj-issued document ensured that her caste, the Hindu system of social stratification, was recorded. As a Kurmi, her ancestors were believed to be descendants of the earliest Aryan immigrants to India and evolved out of the Kshatriyas, the warrior caste but who are now into farming and trading.

For an Indian teenage girl to undertake such a journey, 110+ plus years ago, displayed extraordinary courage, confidence and 'can-do' spirit which is the literal meaning of the word Kurmi. Of course leaving India, the motherland and fountain of Hindu religious beliefs and crossing the oceans - black water (kala pani) was at the time deemed to be losing one's religion and caste. It is testament to the resilience, strength of character and religious conviction of these early pioneers that, despite all hurdles Aajee and Aajhaa and their ship mates (jhahajin) remained true to their faith.

ENMORE

Plantation Enmore on the east coast of Demerara, a sugar producing area, was their first placement as indentured labourers (the system which bound Indians to a particular locality and job for varying periods after which they could either have a return passage to India or settle in Guiana). Within five years of arrival in the country, through hard work and thrift, my grandfather was appearing before His Honour John Edwin Hewick, Acting Chief Justice of British Guiana on 18th September 1909 to "Cede Transport of Lot 1 Plantation Lancaster situate on the East sea coast of Demerary" (sic)', having purchased it on 27th March, 1909 for the princely sum at the time of G$30.00 from Gavin Lova Catto, Bachelor of Plantation Enmore, who I imagine was in some way connected to the plantation owners at Enmore, perhaps as an overseer.

UNITY/LANCASTER - VILLAGE LIFE

Lot 1 Unity/Lancaster, was a large jib shaped piece of land, with the triangular base starting at the turn of a red dirt road running through the centre of the village, almost opposite a Mandir (Hindu Temple). It extended inwards to grazing land and a rice field area then tapering at the end of the next bend in the road, with the government Leprosy Hospital, Mahaica across the road. Over the years this hospital provided work for members of the family and perhaps sowed the seeds of my lifelong interest in healthcare.

This land became the new ancestral home for the Ramrekhas (the original spelling from India but it was later 'Anglicised' to Ramrayka, to make pronunciation easier as Guiana was and still is an English speaking country).

The authentic name might have been taken from Ram Rekha Ghat a holy place in Buxar, Bihar, according to Hindus' scripture and is now a major pilgrimage site.

Several houses could be accommodated on the land at Unity, but the first one, stood on its own for decades. It was the family home where Aajee, as the matriarch, resided with immediate relatives in a traditional Hindu family setting. The home also served as the main venue for celebrating the several days' long rituals for pre and post Hindu weddings (*Vivaah Sanskar*) of various members of the family. For these events the outer areas surrounding the house would be covered with coconut branches or tarpaulin creating a large canopy to accommodate the significant number of guests.

A Maro (altar) would be prepared within the canopy for the wedding ceremony presided over by a Pandit (Hindu Priest).The most memorable part of the ceremony was the *Saptapadi* ,the seven steps where bride and groom commit vows to each other whilst walking around a fire *(Agni –the God of Fire being the divine witness)* with clothing tied to each other, signifying being joined for life to pursue dharma (duty), artha (possessions), kama(physical desires) and moksa (ultimate spiritual release). A most moving and humbling ceremony which I would personally experience and enjoy later in life.

The canopy would also provide space for creating the specialised cooking area - a pit dug into the earth over which metal bars were placed to accommodate the enormous pots and pans which were used to prepare the usual 'wedding house meals' – rice, dhal (split peas soup), aloo (potato), baingan (eggplant), bhaji (spinach) and pumpkin curries and puri (deep fried Indian bread). These meals would be served in large lotus leaves as plates (not to be eaten!) whilst sitting on mats laid on the ground, to scores of guests and anyone passing by the house on the day who felt hungry!

One close relative who always seemed to be in the thick of things, organising cooking and serving meals was Behnoi Ramsukh. He was the husband of my first cousin Didi Ramrattie. Both of them were present at every function and made sure that our visits to the ancestral home were enjoyable. We, in turn, looked forward to seeing them.

An event called Maticore ('earth dig') held in honour of Mother Earth took place on the Friday night before a wedding (there is some similarity to Hen or Stag nights without the alcohol!) Held in separate locations for the dulaha (bridegroom) and the dulahin (bride). It consists of cleansing red dye, turmeric powder mixed with oil (haldi), being rubbed on the bride and groom by virgin maidens. The dye which is meant to ward off evil would not be washed off until the following day. During this period the couple are confined to their respective homes, failing which the purification ceremony was considered void.

The ceremony was followed by much merriment and my abiding memory was to see normally mild manner adult Indian women dancing with each other, one gently pulling up the front of her skirt and twisting it into a phallic form and moving forward suggestively to her female companion. Men were usually banned from the female event but, being youngsters, we were sometimes given the opportunity to have a sneaky peek, only realising years later the true significance.

Holidays and relatives marriages were extremely joyous occasions as they entailed returning to the ancestral home, greeting the extended family in atmosphere not dis -similar to that of an Indian village with chacha (uncles) , chachees (uncles wives) , didi (big sister or elder female first cousins) , behnois (didis' husbands) assembled and being encouraged to participate in these ancient rituals brought from India, some extending into the night, the darkness lit up by gas lamps (as there was no electricity). We all slept on mats on the wooden floor in the house with young male and female cousins (bhaiji and behinjis). Everyone got involved and everyone enjoyed themselves.

The slight downside was the occasional teasing of being a 'town boy/girl' as by the mid-1950s our immediate family had moved out of the village to the capital. To our relatives it seemed that our speech had changed from patois to correct English.

The ancestral home was also the venue at which family funerals, conducted in accordance with Hindu tradition, were held. Unlike most western ones, the deceased would be in an open coffin and, led by a Pandit and assisted by the eldest male relative whose head would be clean shaven for the occasion, puja (prayers) would be said and bhajans (hymns) sung. For me as young boy I was intrigued to see the placing of rice balls (pinda) in the coffin of the deceased and learnt that they were meant to pacify the soul on its onward journey to reincarnation. After the religious ceremony we would accompany the body by foot to the nearby village cemetery for burial or, if the deceased had prior to death so expressed, for cremation on the open seashore of the Atlantic ocean, a 15 to 20 minutes' walk.

Attendance and participation in these thousand years old religious events, brought across the seas from India, and in some instances slightly adapted to reflect the multi-cultural and multi-racial environment of Guiana, reinforced our cultural heritage and our contribution to the rainbow fabric of Guianese society.

In true Indian tradition on my Aajhaa's death in July 1940 he entrusted the property to my grandmother for the duration of her life then to pass it on to her children – sons, Dukhbanjan, Harbajan, Rambajan, Seebajan and one daughter Latchmin.

My dad Harbajan, also called Samaroo was the second eldest in the family but was the first to branch out, leaving the family nest. He married a beautiful young woman, Sundarketaki, called Rosaline from the neighbouring village, Mahaica. My Mum was considered quite modern for the time, being exposed to both Christianity and Hinduism. My Nana (mother's dad) had 'converted' or accommodated Christianity, adopted the name John David and my Naani (mother's mum) Bidyakumari became Charlotte David but, as she and her father (called Berbice Maraj) were of Brahmin caste, she also occasionally did her puja.

"Peter Sahib, your Aajee said that there were other Hindu festivals celebrated. What were they and were they public holidays?"

"Yes Basdeo, These included Phagwah or Holi–a spring festival (although there is no spring, summer or winter in Guiana, its either rain or sunshine!). It took the form of wearing clean, fresh, preferably white, clothing and engaging with similarly attired friends and family to drench each other with red coloured water (abeer) or for the squeamish, with red powder. The colour symbolising the blood of a cruel Hindu King, Hiranyakaashipu, who was burnt alive on the orders of his son, Prince Prahlada, as punishment for the sufferings he had caused to his own people. Another major event was Diwali, the festival of lights, now more generally recognised and celebrated across the world, especially in countries where the Indian diaspora have settled. In London, Diwali celebrations are sometimes held in

Trafalgar Square (a major tourist attraction and a popular public open space in the centre of London where significant social and political events are held), recognising the multi-cultural diversity of this great city.

The night before Diwali, houses were thoroughly cleaned and on the following day, as night fell, several diyas, clay cups filled with oil and a wick, were lit and placed around the house and, in particular, on pathways and entrances. Both of these events signify victory of light over darkness. Diwali marks the return of Lord Rama, his wife Sita and his brother Lakshmana from exile, according to Hindu scriptures. Some British people have commented that Holi, with the bonfire on the evening before the special day reminded them of Guy Fawkes celebrations and Diwali, with lights and presents, was similar to celebrations at Christmas.

Although the majority of Guianese were of Indian ancestry and, the majority in that group Hindus, these two festivals were not national holidays. It took independent Guyana and rule by Guyanese, to put them on the same footing as Easter and Christmas. One wonders why the colonial rulers did not do this".

"Interesting information about Hindu festivals Peter Sahib, please continue with your early family history".

NAANI & MAHAICA VILLAGE

My Naani reminded us from time to time that she was born a Hindu and was of Brahmin caste. However, Christianity obviously had considerable appeal to her as she attended the local branch of the Canadian Mission Church. She wore a hat, not only for attending church services, but generally when going out of the house. This was in contrast to most Indian women of her generation who would traditionally wear orhnis, to cover their head and shoulder. She was married in 1922 to Lochan Singh and after he died in 1940 she never remarried but devoted the rest of her life to her daughter and her three grand-children. Her house and land, blessed with a variety of fruit trees, were sandwiched between a rice mill, whose expansionist owner was forever asking her to sell up, and the back yard grounds of Mahaica Police station.

After our mother died in 1948 we stayed with Naani for a period of time. Living in her house during the time we had a lot of fun amidst the sights and sounds of the environment. On one side of the land there was at times the rhythmic but annoying pumping noise from the rice mill, the strong spell of paddy as the rice was put out to dry on a concrete square, and on the other side the constant comings and goings of stray cattle which had been impounded in a pen at the back of the police station courtyard, patiently waiting for their owners to pay a fine to retrieve them. The fear of falling into the open pit latrine, situated at the side of the yard, also kept our attention very focused. An additional excitement was taking a short cut through the police station yard, en-route to the main road to Helena Mahaica Primary School. At the bottom of the Police Station were tiny holding cells for remand prisoners which were barred and locked but open to view by anyone passing through, We would see the prisoners sitting squat and looking like monkeys in cages. We used to make faces at them and, if were feeling particularly mischievous, we would offer them unreachable bananas. What would have happened to us if one of the inmates had suddenly been able to break out of his cell to catch us was unthinkable.

Like most Indians of her generation Naani was a self-sufficient entrepreneur who not only owned the house and land without a mortgage, but was also a celebrated village baker. She produced bread, buns and kanki (a Guianese delicacy of West African origin, small evidence of the positive multi ethnic inheritance) which was either baked in a huge clay oven built on the premises or, when for some reason that was not working, she sent my brother and I with pots of the mixed raw ingredients to the local bakery for finishing off. This was an onerous task that involved walking along the left bank of the Mahaica River, with the pots on our heads. We made the most of it though by constantly dipping our fingers into the raw mix and have a good and satisfying feed. It was miracle that there was enough left to be baked and I remembered wondering at the time why was it necessary to bake the mixture when it tasted so good raw!

Selling Naani's produce was an early lesson in business practices (which perhaps sowed the seeds for an MBA much later on!). Laden with a basket full of goodies – solara, buns, kanki etc., I would use my childhood charms to persuade residents who lived several lots away from the main road and regarded as 'backdam' areas, to part with their penny pieces or 'jill'. However, I was in serious trouble if the audit of saleable goodies Naani conducted before setting me off on my selling mission, did not match the money that I had brought in.

After our return to Georgetown several adventurous holidays were also spent with Naani, my sister Ena and brother John. We were each given Christian first names. Perhaps Naani and Mum were influenced by the Canadian Mission church and, I felt later, that Dad might have agreed to this because we were living in Georgetown and the names would fit in with the Anglo/African Christian culture of the capital. Dad would also attend church with Mum inspite of his personal adherence to Hinduism. Another example of adaptation made to accommodate city life was that, unlike our village based relatives , John and I continued to call our elder sister by her given name rather that Didi and I did not address my elder brother as Bhaiji. They in turn never referred to me as Chota Bhai (small brother). These Hindu forms of address and respect, which immediately identified the structural relationships within a family group were sadly lost in migrating from village to city.

John had developed particular expertise in climbing coconut trees when occasionally he had to escape Naani's anger. Our belief was that she would have dearly liked to catch him but her dexterity and her generous size did not extend to climbing tall trees! John and I (Ena being female was exempted) 'experienced' how to be punished for serious misdemeanours by being made to kneel on a curved metal coconut grater with irons (normally heated and used for pressing clothes but for our punishment thankfully cool) held by our hands high up above our heads (surely inherited and adapted from slavery days we thought!). We also feigned falling asleep when, after an exceptionally tiring day being ordered by Naani to "mash me feet" (massage her lower legs). As we were equally tired after a day of childhood misdemeanours we thought this was another peculiar 'punishment'. Again all done in good humour (in retrospect but not when it was happening!) with no intention whatsoever of calling Childline (a private and confidential service for children and young people in the UK) even if it existed in Guiana at the time! There were no telephones or mobiles and to complain to an adult would have resulted in a rebuke for being badly behaved in the first place!

In an attempt to emulate to my Dad's linguistic dexterity (and to keep alive our Indian heritage) I struggled to learn Hindi during our frequent holidays in Mahaica. The night school venue was a small building adjacent to a Mandir (Hindu Temple) situated several blocks away from the public road. Armed with my slate and pencil I would make my way to the 'backdam' in the dark, lit by a torch light to ensure that I did not end up in the adjoining canal. The light also acted as a mosquito deterrent. The lessons were not what you would describe as a success, all I could remember were *ka kha, ga gha, na* (Hindi consonant alphabet) and I needed evening classes in London to make up the deficiencies! I was able to apply the additional learning in later years, especially during my time in Pakistan and India.

INTO THE BRIGHT LIGHTS - MOVING TO GEORGETOWN

Dad followed the footsteps of his entrepreneurial parents by leaving the country side (any area outside the capital city was regarded as being 'in the country') and moving with his wife, Rosaline, to New Market Street in Georgetown, to set up a tailoring business and raise our family. Dad was an excellent master tailor who would make full length suits and Indian clothing including a high neck 'Nehru' suit for me as my 'going away' outfit after my Hindu wedding.

Dad remained a Hindu throughout his life but was moderate in his religious practices and outlook. I suspect the reason for this was because we were surrounded by non-Hindus and a Mandir was not readily available for worship. He would eventually marry a Muslim, Bibi Husnara Khan, following our mother's early and tragic death in 1948, at the age of 34 (when I was just five) following an operation in Georgetown Hospital.

So, from an early age we were exposed to the three great religions of the world followers of which, I am happy to say, lived in harmonious tolerance. With hindsight, one of the reasons was the accommodation that had been reached during the early days of Guiana, by the two main races – African and Indians –who shared the challenges of emerging from the barbaric practice and human degradation of slavery and the equally pernicious system of indentured labouring. The races worked together to transform a country of swamp land and bush into an agricultural success which was recognised as the bread basket of the English speaking Caribbean. The land mass of Guiana, at 83,000sq.miles (214, 00 sq.km) and area available for food production being considerably greater than the 12,741sq.miles (33,000sq.km) of the combined area of the 10 British West Indian islands.

Notwithstanding the progress, the dark days of slavery have not been forgotten. Even in 2014 reparations for the abuses of slavery are being sought from the British government by activists in the UK.

Georgetown in the 1940s/50s was, and to a large extent still is, a majority Afro- Guianese town and for a 'country man or woman' especially from an Indo Guianese background to assimilate was a challenge. A shop and accommodation in Newmarket Street, on the fringe of the commercial centre was the ideal place to develop. My father's tailoring business expanded into other areas including a cake shop with a beer garden, dry cleaners and taxi services. The cars were allowed to park, free of charge in the nearby Woodbine Hotel, courtesy of a relative who was a senior manager there - the residual strength of the extended family.

Visits from Unity/Lancaster /Mahaica relatives, especially Aajee and Naani were occasions to look forward to and were always welcomed. Aajee, dressed all in white (as a widowed Hindu woman) topped by a white orhni, would distribute jills (one or two penny copper coins), sweets and Indian delicacies which had been specially prepared for us. The 25 miles journey from Unity or Mahaica to Georgetown in the 1950s was like being transported from the old to the new world. The red dirt road was potholed when it rained, as it often did, and if travelling by train it stopped at every village along the way. Other considerations included the cost (exact amount a secret to us youngsters but we gather from gossip that it was not cheap) and the need to 'dress up when going to town'- Sunday best kapra (clothes) were the order of the day!

Cricket and Indian films and songs were major entertainment events. Mum particularly liked Indian films most of which were dubbed in English because very view second generation Indo Guianese fully understood Hindi (Bhojpuri dialect) or spoke it fluently. However our Dad was fluent because his mother was born in India and the pair of them could often be heard conversing in it. Test cricket was, and I believe still is, the major event in Guyana.

As I recall some schools in the capital closed for a half day on one or more of the five day Tests – a move which was very much welcomed by the children. Despite few Indians in the West Indies teams, Sonny Ramadhin from Trinidad was a notable exception, and later on Ivan Madray, Rohan Kanhai, and Joe Soloman, we all fully supported the West Indies team but when the opposition was India, some Indo Guianese loyalty to the 'home' side was severely tested.

Primary school for me was St. George's Anglican, linked to the cathedral of the same name, reputed to be the largest wooden building in the world. The teaching area was an open plan space situated within the wider floor area of the building with no physical barriers between the various forms. Each form sat separately, on long wooden benches with matching wooden desks with apertures at the front for ink wells. Only the sixth form was physically separated as it was situated on an upper interior level also used as a stage area for special functions. The cacophony of noise was somewhat off-putting, but we somehow managed to learn. The playground was the 'bottom house' of the school, as in common with other buildings in Guiana, it was built elevated on stilt - like concrete structures. A concrete strip, one of the entrances to the nearby cathedral, was our cricket pitch, with a wall of the cathedral as the wicket and the surrounding circular road the outfield.

When my sister and I visited the school 50 years later there were slight changes. Modern seats and desks had been provided. The lay out remained intact apart from movable wooden partitions which separated the forms. They were introduced to control noise levels. An enquiry as to what was most needed elicited a response from one of the teachers that a fan would be welcomed. I bought one and, as I was leaving the next day, my sister, who had also attended the school, handed it over as a small token of our appreciation.

School work was enjoyable and interesting on a personal level. Because we were Anglophiles, we learnt more about Britain, the British Empire and the achievements of Europeans than we did about our African or Asian ancestry. Indeed we celebrated important English events with gusto and the coronation of the Queen Elizabeth 11 of England in June 1953 was one that resonates with me due to the fact that we got a day off school and because we were given Coronation medals emblazoned with the Queen's head and supported by red white and blue ribbons.

Admission to St. George's Anglican School required no overt religious affiliation although we all had to attend the cathedral on Wednesday mornings for an Anglican religious service led by an 'Englishman' (the man might well have been Scottish, Welsh or Northern Irish for all we knew, but as children we did not separate the four indigenous UK nationalities). Another memory during school days was one which I could not fully grasp at the time, but realised it was pretty significant. The British government ordered troops and warships to Guiana, suspended the constitution, removed, the first elected Premier, Dr Cheddi Jagan and locked up several members of his political party because there was a fear of a Communist coup. It was four days before my tenth birthday and sent shock waves throughout the country.

The arrival of a war ship and British troops in the area was also very scary for young people like me. HMS Bigbury Bay, a bay class anti- aircraft frigate sailed up the Demerara River and as it passed within sight of our house, at the junction of Water and New Market streets, with its anti- aircraft guns clearly visible we wondered whether the sailors would start shooting at our house!. An immediate change which my friends and I noticed, as we walked past the Governor's residence in Main Street, on our daily route to and from school, was that sentry duties were being carried out by the soldiers who had landed. We wondered what had happened to the friendly Guianese volunteer soldiers who had previously performed these duties. Seeing The Royal Welsh Fusiliers, The Argyll and Sutherland Highlanders and Black Watch marching pass our cake shop in New Market Street were sights to behold. Some of the troops wore skirts which made everyone laugh because we had not seen soldiers dressed like that before. We were later told that the garments were called kilts and along with musical instruments called bagpipes were proud Scottish symbols.

A widely circulated rumour that caused much concern for a while was that the soldiers mistook the red Hindu Jhandhi prayer flag for Communist flag. We had visions of being carted off – never to be seen again – McCarthy style. Thankfully this never happened as the troops were educated on the flag's meaning pretty quickly.

School life was for me an enjoyable experience because I was successful in most activities, gained confidence in the process and liked the teachers. It was also a shorter experience for me than most because being a so called above average pupil I was allowed to skip form three and obtained the prized School Leaving Certificate which was meant to open many avenues for further education and training.

At the time secondary school had to be paid for and it was not cheap. My sister had started to attend the fee paying Indian Education Trust College and as funds were tight my Dad decided that further education would have to be done through private tutors whilst contemplating long term solutions. This unstructured learning eventually became focused as, following a career review with advisors, Dad felt that the discipline of work, away from the business, and part time study would better prepare me for life, and in particular my ultimate objective – a career in law. Because of the economic situation many Guianese had successfully pursued this path which was considered worthy of emulating.

Government service offered the best opportunity for secured employment – teaching and postal services were discussed as there were potential vacancies for training in these areas. We agreed that I should explore training leading to a postal services appointment. This involved being a 'telegram boy', delivering telegrams from various Post Offices in the city and in the process gaining on the job training of other aspects of postal services. The specific requirement was to accumulate a sufficient number of training days to be eligible to take the postal service entrance examination. Training also included learning Morse code, how to receive and send messages using this system.

Good preparation led to being placed in the top group in the country wide postal apprentice examination. The 'prize' was appointment to the sought after government post of Postal Apprentice. I was provided with full uniform, comprising a long sleeve khaki shirt, with epaulettes and brass buttons (which needed to be polished regularly) serge heavy weight trousers which were far too hot for the tropical climate, and black heavy weight boots. A cork helmet which was also known as a 'bugger house' (presumably named after someone had found bugs in one of the hats) completed the ensemble. It was apparently crucial to wear the helmet at a rakish angle, where the eyes were partly shaded from the sun. I was a little miffed by this because I much preferred dark sun glasses which I thought made me look cool and attractive. Fast forward and the outfit looked like the ones worn by Vietnamese combatants during the Vietnam War.

Aajhaa Ramrekha. Arrived in British Guiana in 1904 died 1940.

Aajee Salukni with Didi Ramrattie (L), Didi Kowsilla (R) and Lily. Aajee dressed in white with orhni covering her head - C1945.

Ena, Naani, John (L) and author - C1954.

Naani, born 1898 in British Guiana died 1986. Wore Western style dresses for all of her life - C1954.

Outside Ancestral family home at Unity (modernised). The permanent structure on the right of the house would have been a coconut branches thatched canopy in 1950s/60s for Hindu functions - 2013.

Helena Primary school. briefly attended this school in 1948/49. The bottom of the building is now filled in but would have been an open space regarded as 'bottom house' - 2013.

St. George's High School – Georgetown. 2013 ('bottom house' filled in).

St. George's High School – Internal. 2013 (partitions introduced to separate the form years).

St. George's Cathedral – Georgetown.

Ena presenting fan to Teacher at St. George's School - 2013.

Canadian Mission Church. Attended by Naani and Mum - 2013.

Backdam area showing Hindu temple (second building left) and canal now overgrown with weeds. No lights at night. Hindi lessons would have been held in an area adjacent to the temple.

Mahaica Police Station. The vehicle to the left is blocking the 'bottom house' of the building where holding cells for prisoners would have been located in 1950s/60s. Grandmothers' house was situated at the back left hand border - 2013.

Hindu shrine showing Jandhi (prayer flags to the left) which would be coloured red and which in 1953 British soldiers mistook for Communist flags.

Ena and her husband John with from left author, Earnest John's father, Dad brother John and young boy - C1956.

Dad (extreme left), Behnoi Ramsukh, (back) Uncle Joe (with hat) and other relatives – Unity village – C1964.

Dad and Stepmum outside shop in Newmarket Street - Georgetown - 1964.

British Guiana Volunteer soldier on sentry duty outside Governor's House, Georgetown 1953. Replaced by British soldiers during suspension of the British Guiana's government.

Dad and Stepmum. – Whitehall – London - 1965.

'Nehru suit' – post Hindu wedding going away dress, made by Dad, a master tailor who made Western and Eastern suits - 1970.

Mum - C1934, in her Sunday School teacher's dress.

Aajee – Emigration pass – India to British Guiana – 1904.

Kitty Bible School – 1960, waiting to be congratulated on being 'saved'.

Behnoi Ramsukh's and Did Ramrattie's wedding – Unity (author baby in Dad's arms back row), Uncle Joe (Dukjbanjan) extreme left, Cha Cha Maga next to him - 1944.

Preparing for Dad's Hindu Shraddha ceremony (one year after his death November 1981).

Dad – 1912 -1980.

With my father sister's children, from left Kumarie, Ramkalie, Baby,Didi ,Kowsilla, author, Roopnarine, Lillolowtee and Bhoopnarine, in Rotterdam, Holland - April 2015.

My cousin Santram, wife Nirmatie (Mavis) and
children, Mahantie, Harindra and Navindra.

My brother's daughter Jacqui, her children Sam, Millie, Ruby and nephew Peter
Ronald at a small, reunion in London - 2014.

CHAPTER 3

THE MIDDLE PASSAGE

SKELDON - MOVING AWAY FROM HOME

To show off my smart Postal Apprentice outfit the government decided that my first posting, as a sophisticated Georgetown boy, should be to Skeldon Post Office, over 100 miles away, at the south eastern end of the coastal road from Georgetown. For me it appeared to be the back of beyond, the other end of the country, on the west bank of the Corentyne River bordering Surinam. I lived alone in a very large creepy house, overlooking the Corentyne River, which I obtained for a small rent as it was not being used.

Not having travelled further than Mahaica, 25 miles away from the capital, on the east coast of Demerara, the posting seemed at first like being sent to another country. However, I liked uniforms, a preference that perhaps started during my early years as an Air Scout which I remembered for the smart uniform and proficiency badges.

I took to the posting like a duck to water. I enjoyed post office counter duties, learning the tricks of the postal trade, weighing parcels and letters, selling postal orders and stamps and the da dit, da da dit, of sending and receiving Morse code messages. I rode around the area on my new attractive bicycle, with white walled tyres, which had a loud tick tick sound, attracting welcome attention.

In addition to post office counter duties I delivered telegrams, to places such as No 63 village (with a beach reputed to be the best in the country) and Crabwood Creek – the last stretch of made up road on the coast, the home of several sawmills, beyond which lay the interior of the country. Although these places were only five to seven miles from Skeldon Post Office, cycling there and back in the heat or through torrential rains, in full uniform, were tasks which I never looked forward to.

My boss the Postmaster was quite a character, formally dressed with collar and tie in the sweltering Guianese heat. He was of African extraction, which was no surprise because at the time very view Indians aspired to, or obtained these senior positions. A jolly fellow who, it seemed, drank white rum and lemon juice at various hours of the day to get him through the tedium of his work. There was also Mr. Ramlall, the postman who delivered letters to Skeldon estate, the area associated with the sugar factory, where mostly Indian people lived, who did not wear our swanky uniform. He seemed to live in an Indian world of his own and on a separate universe and was addressed as Pandit (Hindu priest/scholar). I suspected that he was not an official government employee but was employed through Skeldon Sugar estate. He was a much older man and as a Pandit and I never dared question him, although I was slightly intrigued to know more about him.

On a return visit to Skeldon 50 years later the building itself had not changed, but the personnel and uniform had. No longer were the staff in smart colonial style (but climatically inappropriate) uniforms, with the seniors in 'collar and tie'. Everyone was 'Guianese cool' – black trousers and loose fitting red top (wore outside) were the 'order of the day'. An exchange of 'down memory lane' stories with staff promptly resulted, in traditional fashion, with a photo with one of the charming Postal workers.

Working full time all day left little time for my planned part time studies and after a year the novelty of postal work wore off and one day after returning from a particular long and arduous delivery I decided to call it a day. The long lonely evenings had contributed to my reappraisal of what I wanted from life. I felt that village life in Skeldon had isolated me from city life which I had become accustomed to and liked. Living alone had given me the confidence that I could thrive in more dynamic settings and even wider horizons – England! Not the United Kingdom generally, but England and in particular London!!

Why England?

Well, to some extent it was regarded as a type of mother country, although for some Indian Guianese the real mother country was India. Also as British colonials we were brought up to believe that we were British, well versed in things British (some would say to the detriment of learning more about things Guianese and, for Africans and Indians, Africa and India respectively). We spoke English as the first language on a continent where our surrounding neighbours, Brazil, Surinam, French Guiana and Venezuela spoke respectively Portuguese, Dutch, French and Spanish. We were not encouraged at an early age to learn other South American languages or indeed to learn of their cultures. We were firmly placed in British Caribbean orbit and leaned towards a West Indian cultural identity. Very few Guianese regarded themselves as South Americans. Indeed, I would find out that many people in England thought Guiana was a West Indian island or in some extreme cases situated in Africa, no doubt mixing it up with Guinea and Ghana. The red, yellow and green colour of the subsequent post-independence Guyanese flag, the only such combination in the English speaking Caribbean (which some Indians felt was deliberately chosen by the Afro Guyanese dominated government at the time) adding to the continuing confusion, as the colour combination appeared on the flags of many African countries.

Another significant factor drawing me to England was the opportunity to pursue my ambition of studying to become a lawyer and eventually returning to Guiana to pursue a judicial career. My brother, John had decided to flee the nest a year before and had joined the Royal Air Force and seemed to be enjoying it. At 17 what was there to lose? I had already experienced living away from home in a faraway place. Mum and dad would be sad that another son was leaving them but, in common with other Guianese families, had accepted that wider educational opportunities existed abroad and, once we had agreed to keep in regular touch, gave their blessing to another of their son's adventure!. Secure in this support the resignation letter was drawn up and dispatched. The uniform, in particular the 'Viet Cong' style helmet , was returned, the brand new 'poser bicycle' was sold and the funds obtained put towards the fare, or passage as it is called in Guiana, to England, the 'promise land' of colonials. All that was needed was a passport showing that I was a British subject which took a couple of weeks to obtain. There were no visas, entry permits, evidence of financial standing, sponsorship or other administrative impediments to slow down my departure (all of these would of course radically change in time).

LEAVING BRITISH GUIANA

Getting ready for the journey I was overwhelmed with excitement. I had never travelled on an aeroplane nor experienced travelling by sea. I had only ever been on ferry boats to cross the Demerara and Berbice Rivers – journeys of about 45 minutes. This journey across the Atlantic Ocean would take 14 days. The Demerara River ports in Georgetown did not regularly attract large ocean going vessels and therefore a flight from Atkinson Field airport (name subsequently changed to Timehri then to Cheddi Jagan International Airport in honour of a former President of the country) to Port of Spain in Trinidad was the quickest way to start the trip and a new chapter in my life.

A round of good byes and promises to return were made to relatives at various farewell functions around the country. I would particularly miss relatives from Mahaica/Unity including Naani and Aajee, my father's brothers - Uncle Joe (Dukhbanjan), Cha Cha Maga (Rambhjan) and Cha Cha Seegobin (Seebajan), my first cousins Santram (and his wife Mavis), Lily, Didi Kowsilla, Didi Ramrattie and Behnoi Ramsukh and their families. From Georgetown, there were of course Mum and Dad and my dear sister Ena who had married John Ramsaroop, a legal executive with a popular local Attorney at Law (like many other Guianese many of them would subsequently emigrate to the USA and Canada, as immigration to Britain, was becoming increasingly difficult).My sister and her husband (who had become a Pastor) would build a most successful evangelical and family life in Guyana, then with the Assemblies of God Church in St.Louis, Missouri. Two of their sons, Peter and Paul, followed the footsteps of their Nana (grandfather) and became extremely successful entrepreneurs early in their lives. Peter, prior to embarking on business enterprises, and his brother Robert also joined the Air Force (American not the RAF!). Peter took an active part in the politics of Guyana at one time became a candidate for President of the country. Paul, an IT specialist and philatelist was given the unenviable task by his Nana, of taking care of me in my old age. We are still working out how to bridge the gap between the US and the UK, when and if it becomes necessary! Their daughters Pamela and Vimla have settled well in the US. Vimla and her husband Aubrey, also a Pastor, have successful careers as a teacher and an architect respectively, whilst ministering to an active congregation in St. Louis. Although the oceans have scattered our family we are as close as we have ever been – using significant events – milestone birthdays, weddings and funerals for family gatherings.

It is something of a Guianese tradition for the individual or individuals emigrating to receive a grand send off, with all their close relatives making a special effort to attend the airport and it was no different in my case. More than a dozen people attended including Naani, Mum and Dad, my sister and her husband. There were tears of sadness and tears of joy - sadness from the older folks, because they feared it might be the final goodbye; and tears of joy because those assembled recognised what opportunities lay ahead - not to mention the massive adventure.

As the plane took off I got glimpses of Guiana I had never seen before. The villages on either side of the mud brown Demerara River seemed so tiny and crammed together, soon to give way to Georgetown, St. George's Cathedral, standing out like a beacon with the top of the city trees confirming the garden city title. Beyond Georgetown I got a bird's eye view of the mouths of the Demerara and Essequibo Rivers on their journey into the Atlantic Ocean. The view as we approached the tiny island of Trinidad was breath-taking and when we landed there it marked the end of the first leg of my epic journey. I was a teenager and felt that the world was my oyster.

CROSSING THE OCEAN TO ENGLAND

TV Venezuela was the name of the ship that would be my home for the next 14 days. The route would take me and other UK bound passengers from Port of Spain to La Guiara in Venezuela, then to Martinique and Guadeloupe, across the Atlantic Ocean to Tenerife in the Canary Islands where we stopped to pick up supplies. Then it was on to Genoa in Italy and afterwards a train ride via Italy and France to the French port of Calais, eventually crossing the English Channel to Dover for the final leg by train to Victoria Station in London.

The ship was not the traditional banana boat of folk lore, in fact the only bananas available were those in the dining room! Cocooned together for the sea journey, many passengers, including myself, experienced bouts of sea sickness. Being cooped up with others certainly had its advantages though. I was befriended by a Trinidadian mixed race couple who were taking their daughter, Sherry, to settle in England. She was about my age and we got on famously. We talked for hours and took walks around the ship together. She would be my first 'crush' and having her there made the journey pass quickly. We had lots in common including our aversion to the Italian meals that were served for dinner. Dishes such as spaghetti, pizza and ravioli were alien to us. We were both used to rice and curry and that's what we would have preferred eating given the choice. I recall with clarity (and amusement) the daily evening announcement, in broken English, on the public address system - "For touristic classe passegeros dinner is ready". We never bothered rushing.

Sherry, who was quite sophisticated had a fascination for the French singer, Maurice Chevalier, someone of whom I had never heard. To this day I do not understand why she encouraged me to believe they were related as they were clearly not. I like to think in hindsight that she was trying to impress me. Sherry settled in Earls Court, London, while I travelled around England. We kept in touch by letter and occasionally met up on a platonic basis. This went on for several years and helped my assimilation. Knowing that I had a friend in England who had shared the sea journey with me was comforting (a latter day 'jhahajin')

Other memories of the voyage include La Guiara in Venezuela. After the flat coastal landscape of Guiana, I saw for the first time houses perched precariously on hills and wondered how they had survived the vagaries of the weather, particularly the strong winds. And in Martinique and Guadeloupe hearing black people speaking not English as their brothers in Guiana did, but a strange foreign language - French. I subsequently discovered that the countries were – and still are - overseas departments of France and an integral part of the French Republic.

Leaving the warm waters of the Caribbean we joined the Atlantic Ocean to Tenerife. On arrival it seemed to me no more than a desolate piece of land stuck in the middle of the ocean. It is hard to understand how it has become the popular tourist resort of today. The final ocean leg was to Genoa in Italy where we landed for the train journey through France to Calais for the English Sea journey to Dover.

Reflecting on the relatively comfortable crossing of the Atlantic on TV Venezuela I could not help but thinking how lucky I was to be travelling in this manner. I thought of the dreadful conditions which ancestors of my Guianese country men and women , just 100 or so years earlier had experienced on their forced or enticed journeys, as slaves or indentured labourers, from Africa and India. Crammed into ships that were bursting at the seams, many succumbed to illness and death during the three months journey. Their bodies were dumped unceremoniously at sea. At least they were liberated from the hardships that awaited them.

Landing in Genoa allowed time to travel around the sights and come face to face with the statue of Christopher Columbus in his home city and to hear first-hand of his exploits from his countrymen who were so proud of his achievements. Genoa also gave me my first experience of 'ladies of the night' who roamed around in packs by ships' debarkation areas. A proposition and toothless smile from one woman, old enough to be my mother if not grandmother, was quite a terrifying experience. I recall running away as quickly as my teenage legs would take me.

The train journey from Genoa to Calais was another new experience. Georgetown to Mahaica was 20 miles by a coal fired steam train with a maximum speed of between 30 to 40 miles per hour. It stopped every 15 to 20 minutes at stations where it needed to refill the engine boiler from overhead water towers. It took ages. This journey was 560 miles (900Km) and travelling at around 60 miles per hour it took more than 15 hours, through Italy, Belgium and France. The train was divided into carriages of four to eight closed compartments, upholstered seats, secured heavy doors with an outer passage way. The train carriages in Guiana had wooden slatted seats, in an open plan area and windows which one could lean out of. The entrance doors were permanently open allowing passengers to jump on and off the train at will.

As the train passed from one country to another the border crossings were problems free with perfunctory immigration/ customs checks. The crossing of the English Channel from Calais to Dover completed the lion's share of the journey. All that was left now was the 68 miles (108 Km) train journey to Victoria station in central London. The 4,516 miles (7268 Km) trip from Georgetown to London had taken 16 days. If I had flown it would have taken nine hours and 23 minutes (plus the three hours transit at each airport). Trouble is there wasn't a direct flight then or even now 54 years later. Travel from London to Guyana was (and is) via Barbados and Trinidad at considerable cost and with inevitable delays.

ARRIVAL IN LONDON - THE SOURCE OF THE EMPIRE

The London that greeted me in June 1961 was about to see the enthronement of the 100th Archbishop of Canterbury, Dr. Arthur Ramsey, the head of the world wide Anglican church, whose remit extended to the church of my old school - St. George's. Across the wider world the new American President John F. Kennedy was making his mark in trying to avoid a nuclear Armageddon by advising the Soviet leader Nikita Khrushchev what was and what was not acceptable in the deployment of nuclear weapons in Cuba and seeking a joint test ban treaty.

My brother John, was at Victoria station to meet me off the train and had arranged accommodation with a Pakistani family, in Bounds Green in north London to tide me over until I decided what

I wanted to do. This in itself was an unusual experience as I had never stayed for any length of time with a family other than my own. Getting accustomed to an orthodox Muslim family's mannerisms and practices was particularly challenging, For example being told that I had to be fully dressed at all times because there was a young female family member in the house was an irritation to me. In Guiana we wandered around partially clothed most of the time due to the heat and our laid back nature. Basic things such as having a shower intrigued me as for the first time in my life hot and cold water was coming out of different taps. In 1961 Guiana most families only had one tap and one water supply – typically cool or tepid depending on the time of day it was being used.

I preferred not to eat with the family and as money was tight I ate mostly sandwiches and fish and chips, delicious when eaten fresh, the inner oil protective wrapping encased in old newspapers. For evening drinks, I bought a tin of Ovaltine and rather than boil a kettle I would let the hot water run for a few minutes and use it to make a warming drink. I decided to find myself a job whilst contemplating my next step and as fate would have it I got one, in wholesalers, putting Demerara sugar in brown paper bags. How ironic! I had travelled thousands of miles to participate in one of my country's primary exports and on which the colonial planters had reaped enormous benefits on the back of my forefathers' endeavours.

Within a few days both the claustrophobic Pakistani accommodation and the mind numbingly boring job led to my first and perhaps only bout of home sickness. As I had been a star employee of the Guyana Postal services I decided to write to the Postmaster General of Guiana asking for my job back. Quick as a flash came the reply "I thank you for your letter but having carefully considered your request I regret I am unable to accede... I have the honour to be, your obedient servant, etc. etc." Essentially, I was being told "tough mate, you've made your bed now lie in it!

So I did and never looked back again.

Coming from a geographically large undeveloped country of 83.000 square miles, with a population in 1961 of under 600,000 my arrival in England was quite a sociological shock. I immediately realised I was now in one of the most developed countries in the world. Of the UK's 94,060 square miles, England at 50,000 square miles, was much smaller than Guiana but with a population at the time of 52.7million (that's 790 people per square mile England and Wales) with a net gain of around 353,000 people through immigration. I felt that I would be one of the latter statistics in time to come and although there was no hindrance in entering England minor racialism was rampant in many parts of the country, in particular London, especially against people of colour, for example there were signs in shop windows advertising accommodation but stating "no coloureds… please". A disheartening and obnoxious statement which would thankfully become illegal as more tolerant attitudes were developed.

At the time in America (in particular the southern states) Black people were not even allowed to eat at the same lunch counter as whites because of segregation rules. There were separate areas for blacks and whites in public buildings and on public transport. The Klu Klux Klan were very active and feared by many Black people due to well publicised lynchings inflicted on those who fell afoul of their beliefs. In South Africa, the situation was as bad, if not worse. A member of the British 'old' commonwealth, ruled by a minority of 'whites', who had emigrated from Britain and Holland and their ancestors, racial discrimination was actually incorporated in their constitution. A raft of abhorrent discriminatory laws were enacted against the indigenous people and other people of colour, including Indians. It seemed to many observers that Britain, the leader of the Commonwealth was reluctant to take any urgent and meaningful steps to put an early end to this travesty.

For a young boy embarking on a journey of discovery this was extremely puzzling and came as quite a shock. Here were two primarily Christian countries, UK and USA, the former overwhelmingly of indigenous people promoting equality, fairness and integrity in the countries which they had colonised. The latter made up primarily of immigrants from Europe, escaping all sorts of discrimination and famine, advocating freedom and liberty, treating the people who had helped to build the country with such cruelty and disdain. That this situation was allowed to continue for an inordinate amount of time highlighted the duplicity of their leaders.

Many people feel that the situation still exists in the composition of some international regulatory bodies. For example the permanent members of the United Nations Security Council (four nuclear armed essentially European states and one Asian, also nuclear armed) deciding amongst other global issues, when to intervene and when not to intervene in another country and, if consensus fails, individual members of this select undemocratic and anachronistic group, set up when the world was in another place, deciding to do so anyway. India, Brazil and Nigeria as additional permanent members would bring some semblance of regional, ethnic and population balance but they are still waiting for equal standing – for how long one wonders?"

"Peter, Sahib, an interesting observation, sad and regrettable but unfortunately, that is the way things are at present. Now you have reflected the views of many of your contemporaries do return to your journey".

Air Scout – Botanical Gardens – Georgetown – standing in front of famous Victoria Regia lily (included in Guyana's Coat of Arms)- 1956.

In Postal Apprentice Uniform – Skeldon 1960.

Skeldon Post Office – with Postal colleague in post-colonial uniform - 2013.

CHAPTER 4

PER ARDUA AD ASTRA - THE ROYAL AIR FORCE

FIRST PHASE

During both World Wars Britain relied heavily on her Empire and the Commonwealth both for commodities and human resources. However, there was still a 'colour bar' in place but in World War 2 the British government recognised that help from all quarters was needed and in October, 1939 the Secretary of State for the Colonies, Malcolm MacDonald, announced that for the duration of the war British colonial subjects including those 'not of pure European descent' (sic) could enter the armed services. The 'colour bar' was lifted and nearly 6,000 West Indian men joined the Royal Air Force (RAF) with more than 100 of them decorated for meritorious war service. Knowledge of this contribution to Britain's war effort instilled pride in many Guianese and left a residual interest in the RAF.

By 1960 my brother had come to England and had joined. He seemed to be enjoying his time in the service and I thought why not try it out, essentially as a stop gap to my ultimate objective of becoming a lawyer. To be frank it did not occur to me that I might be killed in action, after all the last World War had ended 16 years ago. National Service recruitment had ceased the year before and although Britain had been involved and would be involved in 'minor' conflicts, and war seemingly continuously, the opportunity to serve the country, develop skills, widen education and visit foreign lands outweighed any reservations I had. In years to come I would see colleagues who had voluntarily enlisted in the armed services and served in conflict zones regarded as heroes. For my part it was an adventure. I was too young to fully appreciate what I was getting into and although I would serve in a conflict zone (Cyprus) I did not regard myself as a hero. Because of age I was ineligible to vote but I could be put in the situations where I could pay the ultimate price! I found this ironic!

A visit to the RAF recruitment centre in High Holborn, London, enlightened me to the opportunities that were available. There were a wide range of trades to be trained in, but it seemed that there was an urgent need for motor transport drivers, cooks, accounts clerks and medical orderlies – so that airmen and airwomen could be driven around, fed, paid and have their illnesses and injuries attended to. Reflecting on the discussions I had with the recruitment staff I wondered whether there were other trades available but these were the ones being pushed to fill the gaps which were being created as airmen were leaving on completion of their National Service (compulsory conscription for two years of healthy males between 17 and 21 years, with exemption for people who worked in essential services - coal mining, farming the merchant navy) from 1949 to 1960 with the last National Service man leaving in May, 1963.

With no clearly mapped out idea where it would take me career wise (apart from believing that it would give me opportunity to study law part time) and, besides my brother, not having any close relatives nearby to seek guidance from, I plumped for becoming a medical orderly. I felt it would be a relatively safe bet, after all, hopefully I would not be killing anyone and, rather grandly, I also thought I would be following the footsteps of one of my great heroes, Mahatma Gandhi who had served as a nursing assistant for the British in the South African Boer War and as a volunteer stretcher bearer in the first World War. Years later I reflected on how such a profound decision was taken, at such a relatively young age, without any great thought about future consequences.

Internationally, the 31st July is a rather significant date for a wide range of events. Christopher Columbus 'discovering' Trinidad (1498), Aurangzeb appointing himself as Mogul

Emperor of India (1658), the UK Department of Health, Education and Welfare being created (1953) and in the USA Elijah Muhammad calling for a Black State (1960). For me the date in 1961 was also significant as on that day I committed myself to military service.

'Signing up' as a volunteer vary widely with some countries having elaborate ceremonies and rituals. In my case it involved attending a rather low key event at the RAF Recruitment Centre in High Holborn for my 'Attestation' a solemn occasion at which I took the following oath:

"I swear by Almighty God that I will be faithful and bear true allegiance to Her Majesty Queen Elizabeth the Second, Her Heirs and Successors, and that I will, as in duty bound, honestly and faithfully defend Her Majesty, Her Heirs and Successors, in Person, Crown and Dignity against all enemies, and will observe and obey all orders of Her Majesty, Her Heirs and Successors, and of the Air Officers and officers set over me. So help me God"

It took all of five minutes... but the commitment was profound and real action was to come.

ROYAL AIR FORCE BRIDGNORTH -SHROPSHIRE

This phase of my life would start in an English town in the Black country (named due to it being a former heavily industrialised coal mining area with scarring of the surface of the local heath rather than the colour of the residents!) called Bridgnorth.

A traditional middle England market town in Shropshire, in the Severn Valley, near to Shrewsbury and Wolverhampton, where I spent several enjoyable weekends. An RAF station was opened in Bridgnorth in 1939 and the following year, during the Second World War, a German air raid killed two women in neighbouring houses. Because of its central location in the UK, rail connections and country setting it was rumoured to be the potential headquarters for Hitler had Britain been invaded. Thankfully, this did not happen, and Bridgnorth served as the RAF initial recruitment training centre, until 1963 when the station was closed. Part of the initial training was learning how to march - or 'square bashing' as we called it. The phrase was presumably derived from the monotonous, stressful marching up down on a tarmac square, willing your arms and legs to work in coordination with those in front and behind you and inwardly questioning quietly, so as not to upset the drill sergeant, why everyone was not keeping in step with you!

So within a month of arriving in London I made my way, thanks to a forces warrant (rail fare) to Bridgnorth and the start of a new chapter in my life. Again a massive culture shock hit me which took some getting used to. The first thing the RAF did was to cut off all my long wavy 60s hair which had taken me years to cultivate (I was not best pleased!). As drilling started, all my physical imperfections were identified and loudly announced by drill instructors who bawled at me as if I was deaf and had crawled from under a stone. The saving grace in this initial onslaught was that I was not alone. I had the comfort of knowing that twenty or thirty squaddies (recruits) in our group would all face the indignities and insults with determination and good humour as we conspired to get the better of the training sergeants and corporals.

RAF food was also a challenge- I had to forget the spicy dishes which I had been accustomed and adapt to mass prepared breakfast, lunch and dinner. As I did not eat beef or pork and as vegetarian dishes were years away from becoming standard fare, I had feasts of beans on toast and eggs done in a variety of ways for breakfast. I prayed for the non-meat options at lunch and dinner and, when they appeared on the menu, I added a splash of West Indian pepper sauce from a secreted bottle, to enhance the taste!

Arriving at RAF station Bridgnorth I was well and truly kitted out from the top of my head to the tip of my toes - every personal item of clothing was provided, including underwear each being stamped with my unforgettable service number (what a tragedy if any items were left in places where they were not meant to be!).

From time to time I am told that I mumble my service number in my sleep!

For the next eight weeks I would become accomplished at regularly spitting on the tip of my black boots, adding polish and rubbing it in as hard as I could. The idea, I was told, was to be able to see my face reflected on the boots – easy for my pale skin comrades but a challenge for recruits of a darker hue.

I would gain expertise in cleaning toilet areas when falling foul of one of the training Non Commissioned Officer's (NCO) dictat and agreeing with my other colleagues that some of the NCOs were indeed born out of wedlock, but likeable nevertheless because there was a secret inner acknowledgement that they were moulding us to become part of a disciplined, thinking fighting machine.

Having enjoyed for most of my life the privacy of my own bedroom and space, a significant adjustment was needed to share a 'dormitory' with twenty young men in what was described as a billet – a long wooden building with beds on either side, a coal fire in the middle and a linoleum floor which had to be kept clean and polished weekly. This was achieved by cutting old blankets into small foot-sized squares and using them as under-feet polishers. Each recruit was allocated two of the following - blankets, sheets, pillows and pillow slips. There was a weekly inspection where every corner of the billet had to be spotlessly clean. Personal lockers had to be cleaned and tidy in appearance. Bedding had to be stripped and blankets and sheets folded into small squares, arranged one on top of the other peeping out at the front, then wrapped around with a third blanket to form a boxed square. Woe betide anyone whose folding precision fell short of the inspecting NCO' s expectation – official punishment for minor breaches of discipline, termed Jankers (corrupted in Australia by their soldiers to wankers!) would follow. This could involve cleaning the toilets, running around alone on the parade ground with an old unusable rifle held aloft – perhaps a real rifle would be a temptation (against the punishment awarding NCO) too far, painting areas and generally sprucing up the camp. Contrary to popular belief we did not paint grass green nor white wash walls which had already been done!

An interesting observation from recruits from warmer climes was that instead of making the bed partly as a large envelope, formed of two cotton sheets covered by blankets at the top and below we would ignore the sheets, as they accentuated the cold and instead make the bed with just the blankets. This practice met with a severe reprimand from the NCOs as it was taught to be not showing strong physical resolve and in any event most unhygienic!

In addition to the usual endless marching up and down we were of course given the full range of military training including how to salute with preciseness, the right arm reaching outwards, bending at the elbow and coming down sharply like a chopping machine, and rifle drill. Those of us destined for the medical branch often wondered why it was necessary to be taught how to use a rifle. Whilst on a firing range, I remembered seeing the fear in the sergeants eyes when my rifle jammed and in seeking assistance I accidentally pointed the rifle at his head. This serious lapse meant I gained further and prolonged experience of cleaning toilets!

Eight weeks soon passed, interspersed with Saturday nights out, travelling to local dance halls in groups to avoid being pounced upon by 'Teddy Boys' who felt we were rivals as young girls were impressed by boys in uniform. Those of us from London or other places far from Bridgnorth wore our smart new No1 uniforms to thumb lifts, on authorised leave, as more often than not we appealed to sympathetic drivers (in particular lorry drivers) who felt that they were supporting 'their boys.'

Passing out after basic military training is not to lose consciousness (this would be an anti-climax!) but the phrase used to describe the final parade when all of the results of eight weeks of discipline, character building, developing people skills and comradeship are put on public display. Relatives and friends are invited and group photographs taken. Sergeants and Corporals Drill Instructors were recognised for not being born out of wedlock after all but being talented, dedicated and hard-working individuals who had formed and motivated the next batch of airmen for the future.

ROYAL AIR FORCE LYNEHAM -WILTSHIRE

Having survived recruit training the next posting was to RAF Lyneham in Wiltshire. I had been designated a 'ward assistant' whilst waiting to go for medical training. Winter in 1961 was one of the coldest in Britain and for me, five months after leaving the tropical heat of Guiana, took some getting used to. Lyneham was quite a change from Bridgnorth as it was a major operational station from which military personnel were being transported to various British bases around the world. It was also a Master Diversion Airfield providing an airfield to which aircrafts could be diverted if their original airfield was unusable because of adverse weather conditions or other emergencies. Several decades on it would gain national high profile attention as the airport where union jack draped coffins bringing fallen military personnel from wars in Iraq and Afghanistan would disembark and be carried from the aircraft with military solemnity.

The nearby village of Wotton Bassettt, which was a bolt hole from station activities, would also hit national headlines as relatives and friends of the fallen and villagers would line the street as hearses passed through on their way to final resting places.

Three months spent at Lyneham flew by as during that time I started to get accustomed to the excitement and challenges of RAF life. The base accommodated a mixture of male and female personnel from a wide range of age groups. Some of the older ones, on their final tour of duty, would proudly draw attention to the ribbons on their uniform which had been obtained through active service in in the Second World War and other conflict zones. They found it amusing to let us sproggs (new recruits) know that they joined the RAF when the country needed them. They would accuse us (with much humour) of joining up simply so that we could be fed and watered. The banter was non-stop, actually – particularly after a few beers.

Unlike Bridgnorth, there were smaller units of accommodation in purpose-built blocks. Food was provided in the grandly titled Airmen's Restaurant (it was assumed that this 'sexist' title would not offend members of the Women's Royal Air Force - in abbreviated form pronounced WAAFs), and it didn't. They happily dined there (political correctness was a few years off in the 60's!).

Lyneham was also the place to I would return, four years later, for a spell of Aero Medical Evacuation Training but in the new year of 1962 I would swap the snow of Wiltshire and the station's bustling air movement activities for the snow and slower pace of north west England.

ROYAL AIR FORCE FREKLETON – LANCASHIRE MEDICAL TRAINING ESTABLISHMENT

Medical Gilt Caduceus, RAF Freckelton

This took place at the relatively quieter but technically more challenging environment of the RAF Medical Training establishment at Freckleton.

Situated between Preston and Lytham St. Anne and around 12 miles from Blackpool RAF Freckleton was previously known as the RAF School of Hygiene but was given its new name in 1956 in recognition of the fact that hygiene was only part of medical training in the modern Air Force.

For two and half months I had a thorough grounding in anatomy and physiology, learned and was awarded certificates in first aid and basic nursing and gained an understanding of field hygiene and military medical administration. On successful completion of the course (which was the first part of continuous professional skills development, I was promoted to Aircraftman with the title of Nursing Attendant 2 (at first a bit confusing as I was on track for medical administration!) and posted to No1 Air Navigational School at RAF Stradishall in Suffolk arriving in April, 1962.

ROYAL AIR FORCE STRADISHALL -SUFFOLK

 At Stradishall I was put under the wings of the Station Medical Officer, Squadron Leader Hobson, who ensured that I kept up with my studies, gave me further practical training in anatomy and physiology, monitored my performance and within a year, I had gained proficiency to move on to Nursing Attendant 1. I was promoted to Senior Aircraftman, a Y shaped three bladed propeller replacing the one blade of a Leading Aircraftman.

In addition to developing knowledge, skills and growing in confidence, Stradishall had other advantages for me personally. It was only five miles away from Haverhill, a lovely market town with a branch of the River Stour running through it. Nine miles away was Bury St. Edmunds, another market town with interesting tourist sites including a ruined abbey. The city of Cambridge was also only 24 miles away. The proximity of these places meant that there was always something to do, see or experience. An occasional perk of the job was to be offered a flight, as a passenger, on one of the Gloster Meteor's training aircraft (Britain's first jet-powered fighter aircraft). The pilots would practice 'circuit and bumps' – landing and taking off, which meant that over time I developed a 'strong stomach' for flying.

Time spent at Stradishall coincided with the one of the coldest winters on record in the UK (apparently only the winter of 1683-84 was colder). Just my luck as a warm blooded Guianese to go through this experience! The Big Freeze, as it is known, isolated the station even more than usual as the roads leading to it were more or less country lanes. But for the fact that the RAF was a major organisation and geared up to handle emergencies, the isolation and suffering would have been greater.

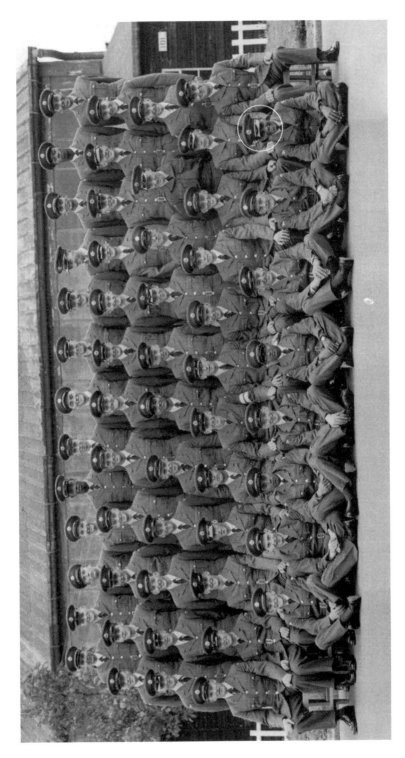

Royal Air Force Group photo – Passing out function – 1961.

In front of No.6 Flight Office – RAF Bridgnorth - 1961.

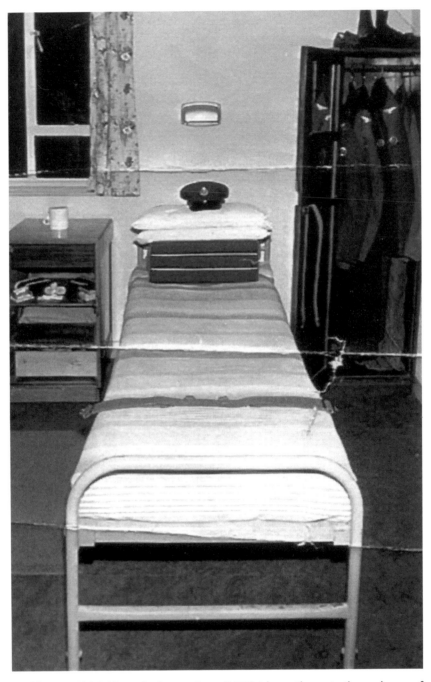

Bedding and kit laid out for inspection– RAF Bridgnorth - note the make up of the folded blankets and sheets pack!

About to clean toilets (Jankers) in 'boiler suit' - RAF Bridgnorth - after pointing the gun at the Sergeant's head incident - 1961.

RAF No.1 Uniform – cap covering eyes! - 1961.

CHAPTER 5

THE LAND OF APHRODITE

RAF SECOND PHASE

NEAR EAST AIR FORCE – CYPRUS – AKROTIRI & NICOSIA

 As compensation for living through the coldest winter in Britain for 279 years, the RAF powers-that-be thought I should be rewarded with an overseas posting. The spring of '63 saw me heading out to RAF Hospital Akrotiri situated in the British sovereign base by the same name in Cyprus. Visions of wine, kebabs and the beaches at Episkopi lay tantalisingly ahead. On arrival in Cyprus I was informed that the old hospital, opened in 1957 was in fact a temporary one made from prefabricated material and the building that I was going to was about three miles from the main Akrotiri station at a place called Cape Zevgari and had just been opened to patients (May,1963). Locally, it had been nick named Alcatraz, because of its relative isolation and barren landscape. It would, however, prove to be an invaluable facility for treating casualties from various conflicts around the world in which Britain was involved.

Within ten weeks of arriving at Akrotiri, I was on the move again this time to RAF Nicosia, the station near to the capital of Cyprus. I often wondered why I was not sent directly to Nicosia. Perhaps being a single airman it was easy to move me around and in any event the original posting was to the Near East Air Force and both stations fell within that organisation. There might also have been knowledge of potential conflict on the island.

Cyprus in general and Nicosia in particular was a coming of age posting both in terms of getting the 'key to the door', (i.e. turning 21), and also the literal opening of a wide range of interests and challenges.

First the interests. Nicosia was well positioned to take advantage of tours to other near and middle east countries. A particular enlightening one which I took was to Lebanon, taking in Baalbeck, then by road to Damascus in Syria and further on the road to Amman in Jordan. I also visited holy places in Jerusalem and, in Bethlehem, I went to the Church of the Nativity, situated on the spot where it is believed Christ was born. A subsequent holiday in Israel presented an obstacle for future visits to Arab countries as I could not gain entry if there was an Israeli stamp in my passport. I needed a separate entry document which was provided by the British High Commission in Nicosia. The visit to Israel, as a young man, was also eye opening as I was invited to a kibbutz in Haifa, a collective community where people worked and lived together more or less like an extended family. Formed in the 1920 by Russian immigrants to what was then British Mandated Palestine it had become a model which Israelis were particularly proud of. Many years later I would become increasingly saddened and disappointed by the continuing conflict between Israel and the Arab nations, stemming from Israel's continued military occupation (one of the longest in modern times) since the Arab/Israeli war of 1967 of parts of the countries I had visited, especially of the holy sites, in spite of several United Nations resolutions declaring the occupation to be illegal.

Solitary journeys to these interesting places caused jealousy in my serious romantic relationship which had developed with Sheila a WRAF colleague. Originally from the North West of England and like me having her first tour of duty abroad. Sheila's hair looked 'ginger' to me so I used this nickname for her. She was not too pleased and, equally cheekily referred to me as Fred, as these were the names of popular motion picture stars. I considered getting together with

Sheila quite an achievement because on the station men considerably outnumbered women, a ratio of around 30 to 1, and members of the WRAF could afford to pick and choose. Our friendship extended to shared holidays retracing my first Lebanon – Jordan trip and extended to Cairo, in Egypt. The relationship became so close that an engagement was entered into, a ring bought and a joint visit made to her family home in England. This produced some funny incidents. Knowing that I was from an Indian background, Sheila's mum had bought a rice and curry pre-packed meal from a super market. It is fair to say that in 60's ready meals were not what they are today and the curry tasted more like pudding as it was sweet and contained currants! I appreciated the attempt to prepare a special meal for me and pretended that I had enjoyed it! I also had the pleasure of attending one of her Dad's watering holes – a northern working men's club and, after asking me if it was alright to do so, being introduced as a Raja (prince)! It struck me at the time that some his friends believed him as they behaved in overly respectful way to me. Others didn't though and it was all great fun. Interestingly, I did not experience any sense of the racial tensions which were engulfing the country at the time, particularly in major cities.

The relationship with Sheila continued until I left Cyprus when, as often happens in situations where men outnumber women on military bases, she fell for a Scandinavian member of the UN contingent! Mortified on receiving this news from her by letter I was determined to confront her in person. I did not have the financial resources to fly out to Cyprus (cheap flights were not available then). I took a train from London across Europe to Thessaloniki in Greece, sharing the train compartment with young people of various nationalities. On hearing of my plight they overwhelmed me with sympathy and 'communal wine' from a flagon which was continuously being passed from person to person (for individual swigs). From Thessaloniki I took a ship to Limassol in Cyprus and a bus to Nicosia. The journey took two days but the mission to get her to change her mind was in vain. The dye was cast, as the fruit from the other tree was sweeter. It took me a while to get over but 41 years later, thanks to the internet and google, she tracked me down and out of the blue an e-mail arrived in my in box and the original Fred and Ginger friendship was rekindled!

Other interests for me included having a weekly spot on the internal radio – RAF Radio Nicosia, playing cricket on sun scorched 'moon crater' ground and a visit from the Air Officer Commanding Near East Air Force who during a short chat and having ascertained that I was born in British Guiana, where at the time there were serious racial disturbances, told me that I should think myself lucky being where I was. I wasn't sure that I agreed!

The challenges were plentiful. Three months into the tour and just before Christmas 1963 serious violence erupted between Greek and Turkish Cypriots who, after independence from Britain in 1960, had settled into an uneasy calm putting on the backburner the Greeks desire for Enosis, union with mainland Greece. On the Turkish side they looked to Ankara for direct involvement and support to secure their population area on the island. Serious blood shed followed the violence with atrocities being committed on both sides. The situation deteriorated to such an extent that by March of 1964 the UN became involved and a Peacekeeping force was dispatched. Part of the British contingent was based at Nicosia and staff of the Station Sick Quarters (SSQ = the Medical Centre), were issued with Geneva Convention identity cards as, although we were not directly blue bereted UN troops, we were asked to visit conflict areas and retrieve the dying and wounded. Our vehicles which were covered with the Union Jack made forays into areas of greatest need, providing immediate medical assistance or bringing back for treatment those whom were badly injured. This heightened tension continued as our Medical Centre hosted some of the formal British contingent of the UN - I believe, 23 Parachute Field Ambulance, Royal Army Medical Corp (RAMC) and other units.

Despite the national civil tensions the atmosphere on the base was good. The Medical Centre was well staffed with a

Warrant Officer, Chief Clerk, a Flight Sergeant, other junior Non Commissioned Officers and airmen. Team spirit was excellent and we all took turn in manning the services 24 hours day. Unfortunately the period working with United Nations colleagues was not given recognition for the usual UN medal. This saddened me and my colleagues at the time and still does. Anyway, the UN peacekeeping presence continued and I was heading for a home posting to Kent.

Via Dolorosa – Jerusalem – Jordan – the route that Jesus took on the way to the cross. 1964

Garden of Gethsemane - Jerusalem - Jordan - 1964. Where Jesus prayed before His crucifixion.

Church of Nativity - Jerusalem - Jordan -1964. Spot where Jesus was born.

With Sgt. Slattery and Nursing Sister – Cyprus – 1964.

RAF Ambulance about to go into conflict area – wearing Geneva convention Red Cross arm band. Nicosia Cyprus - 1964.

Radio Nicosia – Reception. RAF Nicosia - Cyprus -1964.

Episkopi beach –new motorbike - Cyprus – 1964.

Pyramids – Giza – Egypt - 1964.

CHAPTER 6

BACK IN BLIGHTY

RAF THIRD PHASE

ROYAL AIR FORCE MANSTON – KENT

RAF Manston, in north east Kent, close to the coast, was established in 1916 and to start with was a place for emergency landing of aircrafts in trouble. It played an important role in the First World War fighting off German air aggression and, the performance of airmen from the base, heralded the formation of the Royal Air Force on April Fool's day in 1918. By the time I reached there, 47 years later, and after heroic major bomber and fighter activities in the Second World War, it had become a relatively quiet RAF station, still providing facilities for aircrafts in serious difficulties to land but also developing the infra-structure to become a part of the future Kent International Airport.

Life at Manston was extremely quiet, two civilians were included in the staffing of the Medical Centre. One was nursing trained but, because the need for her services was so spasmodic, she became adept at organising the daily tea breaks. The other civilian was the driver of the ambulance , who was a good source of local gossip and from whom I purchased my first car, a clapped out (old) Vauxhall Wyvern, for the princely sum of £30 (an enormous amount of money at the time) and a cherished and expensive bottle of Cyprus brandy. I needed the car to take my new Kent maid girl-friend, Shelley, for day outs to Ramsgate and Margate (nearby seaside holiday resorts) and, because women were not allowed in the Airmen's quarters on the base, as a place to spend quality time. Overcoming these restrictions were also a challenge for me and my colleagues but youths' cunning, together with military knowledge, were used to the fullest extent. These included young girls being sneaked into the single accommodation for overnight stays. They were dressed in Airmen's clothes, long hair neatly tucked in under Air Force berets and fulsome bosoms flattened out with over-sized fatigues. Fire buckets, emptied of sand, were also very useful for emergency use! Discovery of these practice would have resulted in serious disciplinary action, if not court martial but many felt that the dare was worth it!

The routine work of an RAF Station Sick Quarters continued. There were regular morning 'sick parades' taking temperatures, pulse and respiration from mostly young airmen, sorting out those who were genuine from malingerers; carrying out pre- screening for compulsory annual medicals and arranging specialists consultant appointments for those who needed them. Occasionally there were in patients and we would take it in turn to provide 24 hours cover. In addition to our nursing clinical responsibilities, we would also prepare and serve refreshments to the few occasional in-patients, mainly evening beverages and breakfast. I became quite an expert in preparing beans on toast! Refresher anatomy and physiology training included skinning rabbits and examining their internal organs. I found these hands on clinical duties, appropriate for my rank, rewarding but as my interest lay in medical and hospital administration and management, I looked forward to the time when I would branch out into these areas.

ROYAL AIR FORCE – LONDON DETACHMENT MEDICAL CENTRE

Within seven months promotion came, my first Non Commissioned Officer's position – Corporal – two upturn chevron stripes on the sleeves and another posting, this time to London Detachment Medical Section (LDMS). This was the Unit responsible for looking after the health of mostly senior officers of the RAF based in London's Ministry of Defence, and in British Embassies and High Commissions around the world. My base accommodation was at RAF Kenly in Surrey.

The first task was to gently break the news to Shelly and promise, hand upon heart, that the parting would only be temporary as we would continue to stay in touch. The second was to decide how to convey my worldly goods, which by now were gradually accumulating, from Manston to Kenly. Although there were some concerns as to whether the Vauxhall Wyvern would make the 72 miles journey, the plan was to pack everything into the car, deliver the goods and dump the car in some inconspicuous place on the camp. The plan worked , the car not only made the journey successfully but as a reward I decided to keep it for driving around the Surrey country side and also because within three months there was another accommodation move to RAF(HQ) Unit at Uxbridge 23 miles away.

Journeys to work at LDMS in High Holborn, above a café, meant I now became a commuter. Dressed in blue Air Force shirt, black tie and blue trousers with a civilian jacket, I joined the tube at the start of the Piccadilly line in Uxbridge and 28 stops and 60 minutes later was deposited at High Holborn. No free daily Metro newspaper at the time meant a purchase of The Guardian and occasionally the Times or The Telegraph, when my first choice was not available. This helped to develop my political awareness and was interspersed with studying the changing faces and mode of dress of my fellow passengers as the so called swinging 60s – long hair (worn by men not women), flower power, mini – skirts etc. were in full flow.

LDMS was essentially a Medical Centre in London but without any in- patients' beds. It was staffed by retired RAF medical officers– an Air Vice Marshal, two Wing Commanders and a serving Wing Commander - essentially providing General Practitioner services. A team of medical support staff included serving Non Commissioned Officers (NCOs –corporals, sergeants, flight sergeants), Airmen and civilians. We all got on splendidly with little or no reference to rank. In keeping our clients fit and well, we carried out a full range of primary care services. General Practitioners consultations, annual medicals, referring those who needed consultant's advice to the Central Medical Establishment (CME), also based in London, or to RAF Hospitals outside of the capital. The Unit was extremely busy clinically and the medical administrative work to support clinical activities varied and challenging. As an NCO my administrative responsibilities and work load increased and my medical administrative career path became more defined. Opportunity to meet senior members of the RAF, some of whom had played key role in the Second World War, in particular the Battle of Britain, added a little extra interest to the posting. One of these encounters was with Air Chief Marshal Sir Augustus Walker, a Battle of Britain hero, who lost one of his arms when trying to remove an incendiary bomb from a Lancaster bomber. Our paths would cross from time to time as he used an office in a different part of the same building. I was pleasantly surprised to receive a book about Lord Mountbatten's final role as Viceroy and Governor General of India,(inscribed by Sir Augustus) , when the office was being closed. I cherished the book for many years but it went the way of my Air Force uniform and many of my most treasured possessions when in later life I moved houses and others thought they were junk!!"

"That most have caused you tremendous grief, Peter Sahib?"

"Yes Basdeo, but life had to go on and I have tried to cope with it even though it has continued to occur, with other treasured possessions (such as my RAF uniform) in subsequent years, but I will continue".

Working at LDMS was a truly enriching experience. From my base accommodation block at RAF Uxbridge, I had the privilege as an NCO of having my separate room at the head of the corridor, with the remainder of the floor occupied by Airmen. This meant that, at the relatively tender age of 23, in addition to my day time role, I was also a type of residential Warden, responsible for the men on the floor but no longer having to partake in the weekly inspection, cleaning or other tiresome activities of forces single accommodation residential life. At work, each of the four years from 1966 to 1970 saw substantial personal developments. Taking advantage of RAF educational facilities I passed all of the RAF promotional examinations for the most senior NCO's positions and achieved other civilian qualifications which made me eligible for consideration for a commission as an RAF Officer. By 1970 I had to make a crucial decision, whether to leave the RAF after my nine years enlistment had come to an end or remain in the service and pursue an officer's career , subject of course to getting through the officer selection process.

In situations of this nature it is always useful to have a guru (in the true sense of the word for someone of Indian extraction!). Mine came not in the form of a Maharishi with flowing robes and matching long beard, but in the person of a very English gentleman, Wing Commander C.M.C. Smelt, the full time unit Senior Medical Officer (I never knew what his initials stood for!). He felt (as recorded in my discharge book) that "I had achieved as much as any Airman with normal entry qualification could hope for in peacetime RAF" and urged me to consider being put forward for a commission. Working, in London I had become acquainted with many of the senior administrators of teaching hospitals in the capital and felt that the National Health Service (NHS) was a wider ocean to cast my professional net. So I decided to bring my RAF career to an end, although technically I had another three years to serve in the reserves (hence the reason for retaining my RAF uniform) before officially coming off the books in July 1973.

REFLECTIONS ON ROYAL AIR FORCE SERVICE

Reflecting on nine years of service in the RAF I felt that, along with contemporaries, I had been transformed from a teenager to a young man. In the particular circumstances of being isolated from close family and original culture during this 'growing up period', I had done so in a manner which enabled me to share the challenges and joys of young men and women in my adopted country. I had also acquired a British cultural identity, as we passed through this transitional phase together. These formative years gave me a solid ground on which to build on and life-long friends and colleagues. The internet and service associations such as Forces Reunited help to keep these connections alive and I was delighted when two colleagues from my last posting at LDMS, Bob Jeffries and Trevor Steggal got in touch through a Google search.

I was also very pleased when in 2014 I was elected to be Chairman of the Royal Air Forces Association (RAFA) City and Central London Branch to continue to support the RAF family in a voluntary capacity. RAFA's vision 'is driven by the Association's belief that through power and inspiration of its members and supporters, change can be achieved in the perception of society as a whole and how people individually think, feel and behave towards our Air Forces personnel and their families'. The mission is ' through and with our members and supporters to promote the welfare by charitable means of all serving and former members and their families of Our Air Forces'. As an RAF veteran, passionately committed to voluntary service, I am happy to be playing my part in carrying out RAFA's work.

"Peter Sahib, during your period in the RAF there was increasing concern in the country about immigration and a leading conservative politician made what was regarded as a most racially inflammatory speech called Rivers of Blood... what do you know about this?"

"Well Basdeo, it was indeed considered by some commentators to be an 'evil' speech made in 1968 by Enoch Powell, Conservative MP for Wolverhampton, which deliberately sought to instil fear amongst the indigenous population that immigration, and by inference, in particular by people of colour from the 'new' Commonwealth would damage British society and should be severely restricted, if not stopped.

The speech highlighted all the negative aspects of immigration (but none of the benefits) and there was also a suggestion that there should be voluntary repatriation of immigrants already in the country. Powell had the backing of many 'working class' people and it was extremely disturbing (and disappointing) when Smithfied meat porters, St. Katherine dockers and others took strike action in support. A gallup poll showed that 74% of British people supported what was in speech and 69% felt that, Edward Health, the leader of the Conservative party was wrong to sack Powell from the post of Shadow Defence Secretary. Three days after the speech the Race Relations Bill, making it illegal to refuse housing, employment or public services to a person on the grounds of colour, race, ethnic or national origins had its second reading in the House of Commons (Powell was obviously aware of this) showing that at least at a national political level there was a will to go beyond the doom prophesised in the speech".

"This must have been a very uncomfortable time for you, Peter Sahib?"

"Surprisingly Basdeo, although I was aware of the racial antagonism which the speech aroused amongst some of the wider population, I felt that the views expressed did not alter my interaction with my immediate colleagues (including my indigenous girl friend at the time!) and in any event I was slightly immune, from the 'real world' being cocooned in the RAF. However, over the nine years I was becoming increasingly aware of tensions across the world arising from race. In the US two significant deaths had an impact on me - President Kennedy's in '63 and Dr. Martin Luther King's in '68 as both were striving, in their own way, to bring down the significant racial barriers in their country. The architect of Apartheid, 'constitutional racialism' in South Africa, Henrik Verwoerd, born in Amsterdam, Holland, who became Prime Minster of his adopted country, was stabbed to death in 1966 and although it was felt by many of my contemporaries at the time , who had been campaigning against this hideous system of segregation, that it would soon come to an end it would take many more years for this to become a reality.

Another of my wider concerns during the period was the relationship between the two countries which came out of the country of the birth place of my forefathers – India and Pakistan.

I was particularly sad to hear of the passing of one of my heroes, Pandit Jawaharlal Nehru, the first Prime Minster of India who died in 1964 and his successor, Shri Lal Bahadur Shahstri, only lasted eight months before succumbing, it was reported, but still questioned by many, to a fatal heart attack, the next day after signing an agreement in Tashkent, with Pakistan's President Field Marshal Ayub Khan (former Martial Law Administrator) to bring an end to the 1965 Indo-Pakistan war. Shastriji played a decisive leadership role in the war and his slogan *Jai Jawan Jai Kisan* (Hail the soldier Hail the farmer) was recognised as morale boosting call and a key factor in India's victory. However, his real ambition was to promote peaceful co-existence between the two neighbours, a task that is still on-going".

"Thanks, Peter Sahib, for the summary reflections and the issues you have highlighted, I suppose we will now hear how your life has changed as you leave the RAF to go out in the wider world, please go on".

RAF London Detachment Medical Centre, High Holborn – London 1966.

Royal Air Forces Association (RAFA). City and Central London Branch Annual Dinner. Author 3rd left in light suit - 2014.

RAFA – City and Central London Branch – visit to the House of Lords sponsored by Baroness Brinton (sitting middle front row) and Baroness Garden (back row right), author extreme right - 2014.

Settling in to RAF NCO's single accommodation – RAF Uxbridge - 1966.

With Eddie Duke-Low, Standard Bearer, Royal Air Forces Association City and Central London Branch - 2014.

RAF Wings Appeal Collection – Waterloo Station London 2014.

The person named upon this scroll was numbered amongst those who, at the call, left all that was dear to them, endured hardship, faced danger and by the path of duty and self-sacrifice have allowed others to live in freedom.

Now duty complete, they leave their brotherhood.

Let those who come after see to it that this person be honoured and their hardships not forgotten.

Peter Ramrayka

Served: 1961 – 1970

Scroll confirming service in the RAF – 1961-1970.

CHAPTER 7

NEW HORIZONS
GUYANA AND THE NATIONAL HEALTH SERVICE (NHS)

RETURN VISIT TO GUYANA

At the age of 27 I was still single and near relatives in what had become Guyana (new spelling was adopted) after independence from the UK in 1966, were keen to invite me 'home' to find a bride. The Indo Guyanese society, although thousands of miles apart from India, had still maintained many of its customs, one of which was to seek to be matchmakers for their sons and daughters. My problem as mentioned before was that essentially I had grown up in England, understood the culture and aspirations of English contemporaries many of which I shared, fallen in and out of love with English women, on one occasion formally getting engaged to one, and here I was now having to contemplate establishing a relationship with a Guyanese woman who had not experienced the same developmental journey. I just hoped that latent religious and more importantly cultural backgrounds and family ties would enable us to overcome inevitable challenges.

A not insignificant consideration was the desire to please parents and hope that friendship and mutual understanding would blossom into genuine love in the process of married life. The upshot of all of this was that long established family connections led to the introduction to a very beautiful Guyanese woman, immediate mutual attraction, followed by a traditional Hindu marriage - all in the space of three months. My wife and I then moved back to the UK to start a new phase in our lives.

NHS – FIRST TWENTY YEARS

NATIONAL TEMPERANCE HOSPITAL - LONDON

Within three months of leaving the RAF, getting married and establishing a temporary home in a bedsit in Holloway, I was able to use my RAF medical administration experience to secure my first NHS appointment – Staff Officer at the National Temperance Hospital (NTH) in Hampstead Road, London, then part of University Hospital Group (UCH). NTH was opened in 1873, as the London Temperance Hospital, by an initiative of the National Temperance League and was initially managed, as the name implied, by a Board of twelve teetotallers, people who had abstained from alcohol , changing its name to NTH in 1939 and being absorbed into the NHS in 1948. By the time I got there in 1970 alcohol was no longer prohibited, certainly not at Christmas time.

Essentially, my role was as number three in the administrative hierarchy of the hospital responsible for coordinating general administrative activities, human resources and overseeing ancillary staff mainly porters. My RAF career impressed the Hospital Secretary, the title then used for the hospital's most senior administrator, who had some connection with the Women's Royal Naval Service (Wrens) and clearly had some knowledge and appreciation of military medical training and experience. Over the years the Chief Administrator's role in the NHS has morphed, in response to the interminable changes to the NHS management structures. From House Governor to Hospital Secretary, then Hospital Administrator, Unit Administrator, followed by Sector Administrator, Sub Group Secretary, Unit General Manager and more recently to Chief Executive, the latter with significantly more authority and responsibilities with salary levels reflecting these changes.

Within a year a vacancy had opened up. I was promoted to Deputy Hospital Secretary (DHS), number two in the administrative hierarchy. In this role I was responsible, through departmental heads, for all the non-clinical support services in the hospital – ancillary staff as they were described - porters, domestics, cooks, gardeners, telephonists and payroll. Payment of wages to these staff was a weekly task. Each Thursday, myself and a clerk would walk across to the main UCH offices in Gower Street to collect the made up wage packets and bring them to the Temperance Hospital where they would be handed out at what can only be described as a pay parade (in the early days many aspects of hospital administrative practices could be traced back to military practices and procedures as, on leaving the services after World War 2 (WW2) many former military personnel entered hospital services).

No security precautions were taken or considered necessary for me and my colleague to collect and transport the packages from UCH but, for paying out time at the hospital, as the packages were laid out in a tray to be individually handed out, the powers that be decided that the outer door to my office should have a grill installed with a hole created through which the package would pass, to be collected by recipients. The process being that, the clerk would be on the outside of the door calling out the names of the member of the staff and obtaining signatures and I would be on the inside passing the wage packets through the grill.

The ancillary staff, the majority of whom were from Portugal, Spain and Italy found this regimentation, and in particular the grill rather amusing with implicit suggestion of being slightly distrustful of them and, from time to time, resorted to throwing peanuts through the grill if they had to wait longer than normal or if there had been a problem with a particular payment.

My management and administrative expertise grew as I handled high profile tasks such as project managing the move of staff and facilities of a Cytology Unit from the Royal Free Hospital, to NTH's Insult Memorial Wing (an extension originally funded in 1931 by a Chicago magnate called Samuel Insull).

Departmental moves within a hospitals are sometimes challenging but moving a whole clinical department from one hospital to another brought with it the need to ensure the development of robust project plan, effective coordination of all those involved with the move and ensuring that the services provided to patients were not unduly affected. It was an important task for the hospital as it was adding a department that would enhance its status. The move was carried out smoothly and I was congratulated for completing the project on time and within the budget allocated.

Other similar tasks followed including one which gave me an insight into church practices. It was the development of a Drug Dependency Unit from a redundant chapel. I found that to use the ground space on which the chapel stood required the area to be deconsecrated and a bishop was required to officiate. Discussion between myself and the Right Rev. Alan Rogers, Bishop of Edmonton, whose diocese included the chapel, resulted in a most enlightening Christian ceremony, removing the original religious blessing from the chapel, to allow it to be used as a clinic.

Although training and RAF medical administration qualifications had equipped me for the two posts which I had held in the hospital, my seniors thought that I had the potential to reach higher levels in the NHS. To do that I needed to gain a place on a formal structured training programme and pursue a professional civilian qualification. Advice and support came from Gordon Marsh, House Governor and Secretary to University College Hospital Group (responsible for NTH). Mr. Marsh (at the time referring to him as Gordon would be totally out of the question - how times have changed!) would subsequently become a senior member of the Parliamentary and Health Service Ombudsman service. I was successful in securing a place on the Planned Administrative Movement scheme run by North East Regional Health Authority and enrolled on the Institute of Hospital Administrators (as it was then called) Diploma programme. Planned placements included structured periods of time in jobs which would widen my knowledge and opportunities to gain experience in different administrative and managerial posts. I was fortunate to have attachments at the main University College Hospital. Additionally, Mr. Marsh invited me and other general administrative colleagues to his house in Sanderstead, a posh area in Surrey, to socialise which was an unusual but welcome gesture, presumably as grooming for potential senior administrators of the future.

HOSPITALS IN THAMES GROUP HOSPITAL MANAGEMENT COMMITTEE/NEWHAM HEALTH DISTRICT - LONDON

After three years, and with the solid grounding at University College Hospital Group I was ready to move on to the next post.

This was as a Senior Administrative Officer at Queen Mary's Hospital for the East End (QMH) part of a Sub Group with Plaistow Hospital and under the umbrella management of Thames Group Hospital Management Committee/Newham Health District. These two hospitals provided acute clinical services in the area, included in the hospitals name, with the accident and emergency unit and acute in patients beds based at Queen Mary's and longer stay (i.e for older people) services and in-patient beds at Plaistow Hospital.

As with many NHS hospitals Queen Mary's had a fascinating history. It was opened in July, 1861 as The West Ham, Stratford and South Essex Dispensary and in the following years changed its name several times to reflect changes in its role, clinical provision, bed numbers and donations from benefactors, eventually obtaining a Royal charter in 1917 and acquiring the name which remained with it until its closure in 1983 - the land on which it stood was used, as many former NHS hospitals, for housing .

Plaistow Hospital's history was equally interesting as it was opened in 1871 as the Poplar Board of Works Infectious Diseases Hospital and following constant changes, to cater for the prevalent diseases at the time, including smallpox, became Plaistow Fever Hospital in 1901 with 210 in-patient beds. Innovative barrier method of nursing for infectious patients was introduced at the hospital which also provided training for medical students. By 1948, when it was absorbed into the National Health Service, it was treating acute medical cases as well as infectious diseases. Like several London Hospitals, it was damaged by bombs during WW2

The Sub Group Secretary, the number one administrative position, at QMH was David Tindall who as far as I can recall had been there for many years, was in his late 50s and welcomed the arrival of a much younger deputy, who would be supporting him across his range of duties but concentrating on the recruitment of, and support to, junior medical staff, most of whom were from the Indian sub-continent, with a sprinkling from Egypt and elsewhere in the developing world.

My major challenge was to ensure that all the doctors were properly qualified and supporting them as they worked towards gaining success at the Professional and Linguistic Board (PLAB) tests for medical graduates wishing to practice in the UK. Help was also provided as, having completed the attachment and test they needed to move on to substantial House Officers positions. A highly rewarding task. An Indian restaurant near to Queen Mary's provided a venue for drug representatives to offer free dinners whilst promoting their products. They did not quite appreciate that the doctors were not in a position to immediately change prescribing patterns, mindful of their training status, but I suspect that it was investment for the future.

The Deputy Sub Group Secretary's promotion meant that I was now able to purchase our first house, a terraced property in Fourth Avenue Manor Park, on a mortgage for £9,000. Fourth Avenue is not as grand as it sounds, with images of the various avenues in New York! In fact, it was one of a number of Avenues in the area perhaps following the tendency of local authorities and builders giving grand sounding names to housing development projects.

The happy time at QMH came to an abrupt but pleasant end when I was summoned by David Reith, the District Administrator of the newly created Newham Health district, following national NHS organisational changes, to take administrative charge of Forest Gate and Plaistow Maternity Hospitals as Sub Group Secretary. I was thrilled, but also humbled. After four years in the NHS I was being given administrative responsibility for the running of two hospitals both of which were steeped in history. With the role came a spacious office and plenty of administrative support led by Susan, a charming and a most efficient personal secretary. Having been accustomed to hand drafting my correspondence and giving it to a typist, I now had to acquire the skills of dictating to a secretary, who sat with me for up to half an hour each morning going through the post. Susan was also my eyes and ears around the hospitals and alerted me to issues which I might not have been aware of. Another advantage of this type of personal secretarial support is that in dictating a response I could gauge the impact on the recipient as Susan would raise her eye brows and say things like "do you really mean to say that?!"

I found this direct monitoring invaluable and Susan became a true confidante. Some would argue that tying up two individuals first thing in the morning was not the best use of time but I found that the time was well spent and set up the day's activities in a most effective way. In subsequent years there was increasing use of dictating machines and passing the tape on for typing. Yes, these were efficient, particularly for a long report but I have always been, and always be, in favour of the personal approach. Computer technology, several years away would dramatically change all of this.

A tradition in the NHS is that if a family member gained employment he/she inevitably keeps a look out for appropriate vacancies for relatives and, occasionally transforming the staffing of sections of a hospital by people from particular areas of the world with indigenous people being in the minority. To certain extent this was true in certain central London hospitals, as was mentioned at the National Temperance. However, this practice was not confined exclusively to immigrant communities. In Susan's case her mum worked at the hospital and her sister at the other hospital in the sub group.

Both hospitals had interesting histories. Forest Gate was built in 1854 funded by Samuel Guerney a well know Quaker. In 1896 a fire broke out and 26 boys perished because they were locked in their rooms. By 1913 it had opened as Forest Gate Sick Home with 500 beds. – 21 beds for mentally handicapped adults and 25 beds for mentally handicapped children. In 1930 a further change took place under West Ham Council and it became a hospital with 500 beds and by 1937 the number had increased to 723. Bombs in WW2 resulted in the beds being reduced to 201.When the hospital joined the NHS in 1948 it had 208 beds and by 1974 it had been further reduced to 116 and subsequently became a Maternity Hospital.

Plaistow *Maternity* Hospital (separate from Plaistow Hospital) the other hospital in the sub group also had a similar history.

Founded in 1889 by Miss Katherine Twining, who also became the Matron, as the St. Mary's District Nursing Nurses' Home, Plaistow. It developed over the years and by 1923 it had grown to 36 maternity beds plus four general beds and was formally opened by Queen Mary in 1923. Three years later it acquired the name by which it was generally known, suffered from bomb damage in WW 2 but was repaired and survived until 1976 when it was merged with Forest Gate Hospital prior to the latter also being absorbed into the new Newham General Hospital.

Life at these two historical hospitals was quite challenging. Firstly, there was a need to re-establish firm administrative and management control systems and secondly to help the development of clinical association with the London Hospital especially in the field of epidural anaesthetics which was being promoted by a Consultant Obstetrician and Gynaecologist who had sessions in both institutions.

Success in both of these areas led to relatively early promotion, after a year's service, to Sector Administrator , one of the new positions created by the NHS Reorganisation Act 1973, a precursor to many of the organisational and structural changes instituted by successive governments as they battled to promote efficiency and effectiveness in a service much admired around the world. The changes in the 1973 Act first developed in 1968 by Richard Crossman, as Labour's Secretary of State for Health, then modified with the change of government in 1970 by his successor the Conservative's Sir Keith Joseph and finally implemented following another change of government in 1974 by another successor Labour's Barbara Castle. The Act changed the structure of the NHS creating Area Health Authorities (AHA), reporting to Regional Health Authorities. Answerable to AHAs were Health Districts and Greenwich Health District was formed with responsibility for several hospitals in the area. To manage the district Sectors were created. It was a tremendous challenge to be appointed as Sector Administrator for the North East Sector with administrative responsibility for three hospitals – St. Nicholas Hospital, Plumstead (C300 beds acute – a former workhouse opened in 1872), British

Hospital for Mother and Babies in Woolwich (C60 beds – founded in 1905 by three midwives – Miss Alice Gregory, Mrs. Leila Parnell and Miss Maud Cashmere as a maternity home and midwifery school in 1905) and Goldie Leigh Hospital - first opened in 1902 as a Cottage Home for local orphans) To these three hospitals were added administrative responsibility for a number of clinics in the community formerly run by the local authority.

Administrative management of the sector was a particular challenge as a new culture had to be formed in bringing together disparate parts of the health and social care sector, developing an effective and efficient team and keeping the clinical staff, in particular the consultants engaged and informed. As Sector Administrator I had an assistant, who was de facto the Hospital Administrator, at St. Nicholas where we were both based. The two outlying hospitals had their own Administrators whom I visited weekly. I was rather concerned during my regular visits to one of the hospitals as I always found the Administrator sipping orange juice. I subsequently found that there were other substances in the glass which helped the individual to be particularly perky!

The abiding memories of the Sector were that we were able to satisfactorily settle nearly everyone into their new roles and responsibilities. I developed an operational plan, owned by key stakeholders for all the hospitals in the Sector, established the first health centre at Nassau Path, providing primary care services in a new housing development at Thamesmead, built on reclaimed marshland on the south bank of the Thames River and which would subsequently become a major population growth area. The innovative health project which I managed, was led by Dr. Donald Craig, a General Practitioner with drive and enthusiasm and was the precursor to the development of comprehensive primary care for people in the area.

Working with hospital consultants to gain their full commitment to the new organisational arrangements was particularly challenging. We were constantly reviewing the effectiveness of clinical services and mutterings about the possible closure of St. Nicholas Hospital, the main acute hospital in the Sector, caused on going tensions (St Nicholas would eventually close in 1986 and it services absorbed in to the new Greenwich District Hospital)

On a lighter side of events, was the concern of my assistant, an elderly lady and the Administrator of St. Nicholas Hospital who wanted to look after my interest as a younger married man, perhaps feeling that I could be led astray! She kept a close eye on one of the attractive Nursing Sisters from the A&E, who unusually wore relatively strong perfume at work which lingered in an office after she left. This Sister seemed forever wanting to meet with me in my office, bypassing the Administrator, to personally brief me on real or perceived events in A&E. Concern was heightened if on a subsequent visit to my office the Administrator could detect a non- masculine aroma! This would be followed by a gentle interrogation, an assumption that on called for visit had been made by the A&E Sister, and a reminder that I should dissuade such visits! The gentle teasing stopped when the A&E Sister's partner and I became good friends. He was one of the policemen who from time visited the A&E department, with victims of accidents or helping us to sort out drunks!

After two years in the North Sector of Greenwich Health District my performance was judged to be resounding success. I had achieved most of the goals which had been set and had built up a strong an effective team.

HOSPITALS IN LEWISHAM HEALTH DISTRICT-LONDON

My reward was a more senior appointment, one step below board level but with access by invitation when areas within my sphere of responsibilities were being discussed, to the neighbouring Lewisham Health District as Head of General Administration and Support Services.

The appointment also meant that I could afford to move up the housing ladder and the house at Manor Park was sold an attractive three bedroom semi-detached house in Grove Park, was purchased at a price of £19,000. The house was walking distance from Lewisham Hospital where I would be based – so very convenient.

Securing this senior appointment from a shortlist of four indigenous local colleagues was a particular achievement as there were no visible ethnic minorities at that level, nationally or locally, in that area of work at the time. My boss, the District Administrator, Trevor Colloby was from northern England, and was obviously concerned to get the right person for the job and clearly saw beyond colour! Trevor was an engaging personality with seemingly boundless energy, supported by constant cups of coffee and cigarettes (it was OK to smoke in the office in 1977!).

As an Assistant District Administrator I had administrative and budgetary responsibilities (at 2014 prices I would estimate around £100+ million) for one Sector Administrator , two Unit Administrators (who in turn had operational level responsibility for five hospitals), the district heads of supplies, catering, laundry, central sterile supply services (CSSD), and domestic services. The District Pharmacist, Naaz Coker also attended my heads meeting although reporting responsibility for her services rested with an Area Pharmacist. Naaz would go on to Chair the Refugee Council, St. George's Healthcare Trust and win the prestigious Asian Women Achievement Award for 2004.

Again all the hospitals were steeped in history – the sector, all within the south east London Borough of Lewisham, comprised Lewisham Hospital which came into being in 1612 as workhouse but was formally founded in 1894. In the First World War it became the Lewisham Military Hospital and in WW 2 it was hit by V-1 flying bombs. In the following years the hospital expanded and by 1968 it had become the first district general hospital in England to have an Intensive Care Unit.

St. John's Hospital, then linked, started its life in 1884 under the auspices of a Nursing Sisterhood of St. John the Divine, damaged nine times during WW2. It looked after casualties from the 1957 train crash at St. John's railway station when 92 people were killed and 173 injured. Sydenham Children's Hospital, the third of the sector's three hospitals, opened in 1872 by Miss Edith Elwes as a Home and Infirmary for Sick Children and South London dispensary for women. Hither Green Hospital, separately managed was opened by the Prince of Wales in 1897 as a fever hospital following an epidemic of scarlet fever in 1892-93 and at the time was the largest fever hospital in England, it was bombed during WW2 and took casualties from the infamous train crash at Hither Green in 1967 which resulted in 53 deaths and 90 people being injured. Grove Park Hospital with its own Unit Administrator, Ingrid Craig, a most competent and professional young lady, who like me was breaking through the colour bar, albeit at a lower level! The hospital started its life as a workhouse in 1902 changed it clinical usage several times, requisitioned in WW1 by the Army Service Corps and in WW2 was damaged by high explosive bombs. Two nurses Mary Fleming and Aileen Turner were awarded George Medals for saving trapped patients.

At age 34 I now had substantial management and leadership responsibilities for eight professionally qualified and highly skilled senior managers and collectively we had to ensure that all the non-clinical supporting services across the health district were provided in timely an efficient manner. As would be constant themes throughout my NHS life, budgetary concerns, staffing issues and rationalisation of services to reflect clinical changes predominated.

My first major challenge in the new post came with the 1978-79 'Winter of Discontent' - the bitter and intense industrial disputes leading to widespread strikes by public sector unions. Membership was strong amongst significant sections of the ancillary staff – in particular amongst porters, domestic assistants (cleaners) and catering staff. As the largest hospital in the group and sited on a main access road, Lewisham Hospital was the centre of attention in the area and hotbed of militancy. Actions were led by a shop steward who was anxious to demonstrate solidarity with the wider national trade union movement. Management's challenge was to emphasise that locally we could not change the nationally negotiated conditions of service, especially pay increases which the government was trying to keep below 5% as one of the measures to control inflation. As the senior manager dealing with the Unions my immediate task was to persuade the local trade union leaders not to block the entrance to the hospital. Restricting services to just accident and emergencies was a tactic being applied or contemplated elsewhere in the country, largely in support of trade unionist in other public service sectors who were taking all out strike action. To a large extent we were able to contain local action by tactical local compromises. One of which was to allow black refuse bags to pile high outside the main Lewisham hospital entrance which would show passing motorists that hospital workers were supporting the national action. In turn motorists would toot their horns, all attracting local newspaper publicity. At the end of the day (and in the dark) most of the bags would be removed and incinerated ready for another load the next day. It is a testimony to the good industrial relationship which I had developed between staff and management that the hospitals in the group remained open throughout this extremely difficult period.

Life in Lewisham Health district was not only strengthening my senior managerial skills but exposing me to the shenanigans that constant national political interference by Secretaries of State of Health (SofSH) brings to the operational management of the health services and in particular at the time local health authorities. Lewisham was part of Lambeth, Lewisham and Southwark Area Health Authority (Teaching – AHA(T)) and the then Health Secretary , Patrick Jenkins, a Conservative politician decided to dismiss the Authority on the 1st August 1979 because he feared that the Authority would not keep to its spending limit for 1979-80. He then appointed Commissioners to run the services.

His action was subsequently judged by the High Court to be invalid and what was publicly described as a 'crawling apology to the House of Commons' he admitted that he was wrong. He reinstated the Authority from 1st April 1980 and had to introduce another Bill to cover all the invalid actions which had been taken by the Commissioners to avoid a raft of compensation claims (25 years later again with Lewisham Hospital clinical services being at centre stage, yet another Conservative Health Secretary, Jeremy Hunt, took action, the results of which would have severely curtailed services at the hospital. His decision was also taken to the High Court and was also overturned).

Top management by Commissioners instead of by the AHA was an interesting experiment as the four District Administrators heading the Health Districts in the Area -John Carrurthers from Guy's, John Collinson from King's, John Wyn Owen from St. Thomas' and John Thompson (who had by now replaced Trevor Colloby) from Lewisham would have meetings with the five Commissioners on a regular basis and the feed-back we had from our John, a former decorated WW2 veteran with a Distinguished Flying Medal, noted locally for his calmness, integrity, love for the democratic process and dry humour, was that the four Johns meetings, were very business-like with none of the AHA's democratic involvement of local politicians and the public!

Consensus management, shared responsibility at the top level for managing the health services, was the order of the day but the Conservatives relentless action to change this, would see another reorganisation bubbling up as the Thatcher years embedded and continuation of the constant bashing of 'administrators' who were portrayed as the bogey men (and at the time to a lesser extent bogey women) even though the politicians inevitably relied on them to implement their constantly 'new broom sweeps clean' changing strategies and decisions.

At work despite the constant criticism of a surplus of 'Administrators' in fact at the top level of the health district there were only three. The District Administrator and two Assistants - me for Support Services and the other for Planning- the latter with a small team of two including, Patricia Riordan, a brilliant young graduate from northern England.

Arriving with a BA and an MA she impressed us all with her quick grasp of key issues and her potential for advancement in the service. After a successful time in the District she left, gained a PhD then, following graduating as a clinical doctor, have excelled in her field. One example, but a reflection of the intellectual capacity of people aspiring to top level management positions in the NHS.

Another period of NHS restructuring started in 1982. The Area tier, which had been dismissed then reinstated locally had now been abolished across England and Wales and replaced with 192 District Health Authorities (DHA).The 14 Regional Health Authorities (RHA) formed following the last major reorganisation in 1974 remained as did the 90 Family Practitioner Committees (FPC) and seven Special Health Authorities with responsibility for managing London's Postgraduate teaching hospitals.

The main impact for the senior management/ administrative cadre was that we no longer had a job! The new posts were put in a geographical pool and a matching process was initiated through which selection was based on preferences expressed by applicants and 'fit' by the new employing authorities. Lewisham had become Lewisham and North Southwark Health District (L&NS) bringing together Lewisham and Guy's Hospital. The first circle on the merry go round saw most of the Area Administrators being appointed, some would say being slotted in to the new District Administrators posts. For L&NS it was the former Area Administrator of Kent.

Five years at Lewisham meant that I either had to apply (and be successful) for one of the existing senior positions in the new Health District or failing that seek opportunities elsewhere. Lewisham was obviously my first choice mindful of the reputation which I had built up locally, in particular with the trade unions, during the winter of discontent. Somewhat to my surprise my first choice did not match the new employer's 'fit' and I was subsequently appointed to one of my other choices, Dartford and Gravesham Health District to which the District Administrator of Guy's, John Carruthers had also been appointed.

The local trade unions had considerable anxiety about the organisational changes. They saw them as another example of wasting resources on organisational structures, money which could be better spent by focusing directly on front line clinical care. Locally there was also a widely held suspicion that this was an opportunity to displace senior management who had good relationships with the unions. They took umbrage and mounted protests against my non appointment. Whilst silently deeply humbled and appreciative of the Union's support for me I was careful not to become involved in career limiting actions. I was pleased when on my appointment to a new post my existing authority issued a statement that I was not discriminated against but was appointed to a similar senior position in a neighbouring organisation – Dartford and Gravesham Health Authority.

HOSPITALS IN DARTFORD AND GRAVESHAM HEALTH AUTHORITY-KENT

Dartford and Gravesham Health District brought two disparate areas together. Dartford, in Kent, is amongst other things now widely known for the magnificent Queen Elizabeth II bridge, 449 ft. (137m) high and 2,264ft (812m) long spanning the Thames River and joining the two ends of the outer London ring road, the M25 motorway, bringing parts of the counties of Kent and Essex together. Gravesham's principal town is Gravesend and the borough includes a number of parishes with quintessential English villages.

The health district headquarters were at Darenth Park Hospital, just outside of Dartford. The hospital was opened in 1897 as the Darenth School for Imbecile Children. The Gothic style building cost £88,750 pounds and could accommodate 580 children. Over the years other building were added to the site and by 1921 it had 1668 beds and was renamed Darenth Training Colony. So described because the colony comprised of 103 acres of arable land and 46 acres of grassland and was self-sufficient in food produced on the farm and to a certain extent was also self-contained.

Expertise in treatment of mentally handicapped children and adults led to many changes both in the type of clinical services being provided and accommodation to meet the needs. Children stopped being admitted to the Colony in 1935 and two years later it was renamed Darenth Park Hospital. By 1948 when it joined the NHS it had 2260 beds.

In 1982, when I joined, a major decision had already been taken, nine years ago, to close the hospital. Bed numbers had risen to over 2000 in 1954 then fallen to around 700 as learning disability patients were being discharged into communities in south east London, Kent and Sussex, original places from where the patients were admitted, although some had lived in the hospital for over 40 years. This decision was taken as one of the best ways of dispersing the patients in the communities and to lessen the impact on any particular Local Authority having to cope with a large influx of learning disabilities discharges

My new role in the district was broadly similar to that in Lewisham. As the Assistant District Administrator, I was responsible for the headquarters functions of the non-clinical support services and supported the Unit Administrators of five hospitals - Joyce Green, West Hill, Stone House and Mabledon, North West Kent and, in particular Darenth Park. Darenth because of its national high profile status as the first major learning disability retraction programme in the country to gradually discharge all of its patient into the community and close the hospital. Although the strategy was being led by the Region and in particular by the Regional Nursing Officer, Audrey Emerton(who was later on appointed a Dame then made a life Peer), operational delivery required an efficient team and excellent work was done by Pauline Stanley a senior nurse. The smooth 'run-down' and closure of the hospital in 1988 was a credit not only to the Regional and District Management Teams but also to the sterling work done by the Darenth Park team some of whom had seen the programme through from start to finish. The task to retract, disperse the residents and close Darenth became a subject for academic research, publication of books and a model for subsequent long stay hospital closures throughout the country. Managing staffing relations was also particularly trying and was handled very well by the Personnel Department, as Human Resources (HR) were generally described at the time. It gave up and coming HR specialists a solid grounding and one who particularly excelled, Beverly Ashby, was able to move on to run her own department at Joyce Green Hospital, in the District, and eventually to more senior positions in private healthcare becoming an Executive, Leadership and Development Coach and a Mediator. Another example of the quality of NHS non clinical staff.

Closing Darenth was conducted during the process of further major national NHS organisational upheaval. Consensus management, the system by which the health district was managed by six multi discipline professionals, a District Management Team comprising one representative each from consultants and General Practitioners, community physician, chief nurse, chief administrator and a treasurer, was replaced in 1984 by general management.

Proposed by Sir Roy Griffith, Deputy Chairman of Sainsbury's one of the top supermarkets in the UK. He had been brought in by Prime Minister, Mrs. Thatcher in 1983 to 'produce a report on the management of the NHS'. General management advocated one individual at each tier of the NHS to have responsibility, authority and accountability for planning and implementing decisions, flexibility in team structures and greater emphasis on leadership. Implementation of general management meant that once again the top tiers had to change. Regional, District and Unit General Manager would be new titles and they would be given the authority recommended in the Griffiths Report as the top manager of the corresponding tiers of the NHS.

Administrators who, because of their co-ordinating role, were grudgingly regarded, as the defacto leaders of the team or first amongst equals, and others who felt qualified had to apply for these posts which after the first round, seeking internal candidates, were open to anyone. Within the South East Region appointments to District General Manager posts included senior military officers - a Rear Admiral, an Air Vice Marshal, a Brigadier plus an array of commercial and industrial people who felt, and were supported by appointing authorities, that their experience of senior or top management in other fields were directly transferable to the managerial cultural setting of the NHS. The fact that most of them left after a relatively short space of time is evidence of the peculiar nature of leadership in the NHS where a combination of institutional knowledge, cultural fit, empathy, some would say vocational commitment and public sector ethos predominate.

In Dartford and Gravesham we had Tony Marchant a former accountant with Dunlop Rubber Company and a Director of ICI. Soon after his appointment as District General Manager he sought to steady the ship. As the previous District Administrator had left and I was fulfilling the role as acting DA, he decided to recommend my appointment to the substantive District Administrator's position. I subsequently learnt that the Region were not too pleased that a substantive appointment was being made whilst the new organisational structure was being worked through but as it would take nearly a year for this to be done the local decision remained intact, perhaps indicating the new authority of the Chairmen and the DGMs.

My substantive appointment as District Administrator in 1985 was welcomed by many locally and wider a field as I was the first person in the country from a visible ethnic minority to obtain this much coveted position. Although the NHS had recruited ethnic minorities as doctors and nurses, and to fill catering, domestic and portering duties, administration and general management leadership role at the time either did not appeal to ethnic minorities or the prevailing national culture dissuaded those who were so inclined, in the belief that they were unlikely to succeed because of the perceived colour barrier. To a certain extent the barrier would be slightly indirectly raised when, with the constantly changing of the structures of the NHS, there was an influx of ethnic minorities (mainly doctors from the Indian sub- continent) in leadership roles, as Chairpersons of new Primary Care Groups and their successor Primary Care Trusts. These were non- executive appointments but hugely important in providing leadership in a changing environment.

Within a year the new general management structure had been developed and it was time for title changes. Most members of the District Management Team acquired positions as Board Directors and I became Director of Administration, Personnel and Estate Management, Secretary to the Authority and Deputy District General Manager. A mouthful, but it embraced district level responsibility for the district heads of services, as well as running the administrative functions of the Health Authority, deputising for the DGM and supporting elected members who now included a wide range of local community representatives as well Councillors from Dartford, Gravesend and Kent County Council, the Vice Chairman, Edward (Teddy) Moore, coming from the latter body.

The first chairman of the Authority in 1982 was Dr. George Stratton, a former consultant physician whose links with the area went back to 1946 when he was appointed as a medical specialist. He was followed in 1988 by Tim Brinton, a former Conservative

MP for Gravesham and a former broadcaster with BBC and ITV. George provided considerable clinical and local knowledge of the area and Tim brought considerable media and political expertise. Meetings were held in the public although on most occasions 'the public' consisted of two or three people (unless on the agenda there was an item to radically change the clinical services or close a hospital when attendance would swell to dozens).

As District Administrator then Director of Administration I was the spokesman for the Health Authority and formed cordial relationships with the media. In terms of stories, there were always rich pickings to be had from the goings-on within the local health service; particularly anything that affected patient care directly. It was my job to deal with the individual journalists when they contacted us to either obtain factual information or to give the authority the opportunity to comment if they'd sourced a story themselves. Although (obviously) I was expected to be open and honest, it was also crucial for public relations that I handled matters diplomatically and sensitively. I was no spin doctor, but I obviously did my best to present information in the most positive light possible. Luckily this approach came naturally to me, it was common sense as far as I was concerned and there were many occasions when I was able to reduce the impact of a 'bad' story. The flip side of the coin was that I was able to pro-actively promote things the authority wanted the public to know about. Results included the launch of 'Health Matters' a free occasional insert in the main local newspaper, Kentish Times, following an agreement I had reached with the Editor to provide health stories which would be of interest to readers.

Inevitably, some reporters were better and easier to get on with than others. One in particular worked for Kentish Times, and she became a regular feature at meetings, briefings etc. Her name was Aylia Fox. She was young, smart, professional and attractive. Over time we became friendly as I was drawn to her engaging personality and work ethic, a friendship that has continued to the present time and I was flattered to be asked to be the Godfather to her daughter Sienna, now 14 years old, which I accepted.

I am also close to her family and know her mother Jennifer well. Although she now lives in the Lake District, we keep in touch by phone and send birthday/Christmas cards etc. Jennifer is also a published author and I have had great pleasure reading her books.

In the same way that my career had taken off, so too did Aylia's. She had a drive and determination that was clear for all to see. Her ambition was to work on a national newspaper and even before she had finished her formal journalism training, she was doing Saturday shifts on the famous (now defunct) News of the World. When she was just 22 she was taken on there as a staff journalist and remained in her job for nearly nine years. She was responsible for some of the paper's biggest stories including the high profile (and controversial) one about a woman called Mandy Allwood who became pregnant with eight babies. She was also appointed medical correspondent and Midlands' Editor during her tenure.

After that, she became a producer for morning TV news show GMTV, and when her daughter was one-year-old, she went back to work as an Editor on a local newspaper in Luton at which she was most successful. She also wrote an educational book and became a media pundit on both TV and radio. She once presented the highly respected media show, What the Papers Say.

I had always known Aylia was destined for bigger and better things. This view was partly prompted by an incident when she was driving my car (with me in it) and we skidded on black ice while going round a corner. We crashed and as the car turned over a couple of times and came to a stop perilously closely to the edge of a motorway bridge, I felt my life flash in front of me (yes, it really does happen!). Luck was on our side though. Neither of us was injured; just battered, bruised and shocked. The car, however, was severely damaged in particular the front and roof and was written off.

The next day Aylia informed me that she'd written a story about it for the paper she was, at that time, chief reporter of – the Swanley Times.

I was aghast as I imagined headlines along the lines of: "Local NHS Chief Narrowly Escapes Death in Horror Smash." Not only did I not want the embarrassment of the publicity, but I realised it would not be good for the public's perception of impartiality as far as the Authority's relationship with the press was concerned. I did the only thing I could think of – I contacted Aylia's Editor and managed to get the story pulled.

I was pleased. Aylia was not. We laugh about it now, but at the time it was almost a deal-breaker for our friendship.

Aylia's now 49 and has had a complete career change. She retrained and now runs her own business as a personal trainer. She's super-fit and very good at what she does. She has offered to train me, but I have politely declined fearing our friendship might not survive the process.

"Peter Sahib, obviously a very gifted young woman but why have you continued being a friend after she crashed your car, surely you should have considered ending the relationship after that?"

"Not really Basdeo, it was an accident! We continued to work harmoniously while in Dartford and as mentioned we have stayed in touch over the years. Now if you don't mind I will get on with my time at Dartford and Gravesham"

The Health Board wrestled with the usual challenges that have always dogged health services over the years –matching resources to meet changing demand, motivating staff (in particular keeping clinical consultants informed and engaged), constant scrutiny from an increasingly informed public and in particular from local and national politicians, promoting efficiency and innovation and developing good working relationship with the local media, notwithstanding the above average relationship which I had already developed with one particular reporter.

The national recognition for the closure of Darenth Park was an achievement which we were particularly proud of, as was carrying out the rationalisation of clinical services across the district which would lead to the creation of a plan to develop a District General Hospital for the area. Well attended consultation meetings were held in village halls, hearing first hand from users of the services and adapting our plans to reflect what we had heard. Proposed closure of several of much loved local hospitals generated considerable concern but the plans which we had started to develop would eventually lead, several years later, to the development of the controversial first Private Finance Initiative (PFI) hospital in the UK – Darent Valley. Another first for the area but one which would lead to much soul searching later on.

Resources are forever a challenge and we hit national headlines when it was alleged that the lights at Joyce Green Hospital were about to be switched off because we could not pay the bill! Sensational, but quite inaccurate. Yes, the district was experiencing financial difficulties but we could pay our bills and in any event it was unthinkable that electricity serving a hospital would be cut off. As the Authority's spokesman, skilful handling of follow up enquiries ensured that the story was eventually put to rest.

Another serious event occurred on the night of 15th-16th October 1987 when a severe storm, some referred to it as a mini hurricane, hit the Greater London area and caused devastation to buildings with trees falling on hospital roofs across the health district. Prompt remedial action by the estates department, one of my principal areas of responsibility, ensured that power was quickly restored, emergency repairs carried out and effects on patients were minimal. Rare trees and shrubs at Joyce Green Hospital, which were provided many years ago due to the connection of one of the head gardeners and the Royal Botanical Gardens at Kew were unfortunately lost forever.

Managers in the NHS often come in for wild and in many cases unfounded criticisms from those who see them as people employed to put obstacles in the way of effective healthcare. But they fail to recognise that, in fact, managers are enablers - providing the infrastructure and support to keep the organisation efficient, effective and looking out for opportunities to promote innovation.

'Pioneer Clinic to be proud of... 'was the headline in the local newspaper, Kentish Times, announcing the innovative joint venture between myself and Colin Rodden, the Town Clerk of Swanley Town Council to provide a £400,000 state of the art clinic called 'The Oaks'. It brought a range of community services to the people in the area. The working together of Health and Local Authority

with a four doctor partnership was early evidence of collaboration which continues to be a challenge in present day health care.

After eight years in the district, five of which were spent at the top management table, what had I achieved? I was personally proud that I had led some major development projects - a College of Healthcare Studies, an Intensive Care Unit at Joyce Green Hospital and, Archery House, a facility for remaining learning disability residents from Darenth Park hospital who needed continuing care in domiciliary setting as they could not be returned to their original home of domicile. In addition I had satisfactorily managed multi-million budgets, mentored and supported senior managers across the district who, in turn were responsible for hundreds of staff and had led or contributed to the development strategies of the Health Authority.

Moving on to pastures new was recorded by the Kentish Times with the headline - *"Health chief leaves for job In Botswana"* adding in the opening paragraph of the article that "the man who has helped shaped the district's health service set off last weekend to work in the third world" and later on" he has helped to influence many of the decisions of the health authority and believes there have been significant improvements in patient care". With these warms words and the customary send- off party thrown by friend and colleagues I was ready for my new adventure. A tie with the Gravesend motto, and a ghetto blaster were amongst the parting gifts!

I could not leave Dartford without recording the unsolicited letter that I had received from Debrett's, the specialist publisher. Founded in 1769 to publish the names and family history of Peers and Baronets but which has since broadened to include those whose achievements are noteworthy. On receiving the envelope my immediate thought was:

"Had I made the grade, am I to be ennobled?" Alas, this was not the case!

A lesser recognition was that there was going to be a publication called 'Debrett's People of Kent' recognising people of importance working or living in the county and I was being requested for information to be included. I responded positively and in the 1990 edition there I am at page 152, Ramrayka P, JP, listed between Rampton, Sir Jack Leslie, KCB and Ramsay, Col. Gorge Patrick Maule.

"Peter Sahib, not bad for a humble healthcare director and ex-corporal – listed between a Knight and a Colonel!"

"Thanks Basdeo, I will take that as a congratulatory comment, here is a banana and I will carry on with my reflections"

REFLECTIONS ON FIRST TWENTY YEARS IN THE NHS
Reflecting on twenty years services in the NHS I felt that my nine previous years in RAF medical branch, especially the last four years at London Detachment Medical Centre, had provided a solid ground on which to build new skills and experience.

Selected and sponsored for 'a potential top manager's' Masters in Business Administration course, was confirmation that the NHS had continued to recognise my potential and was prepared to invest in me. I needed to repay that confidence and set about giving to the programme the commitment it deserved.

After a full day's work, many of which were challenging and on occasion mentally exhausting, I drove twice a week from Dartford to the Polytechnic of Central London/ University of Westminster campus in Marylebone, central London, a distance of 20 miles (but could take anything up to 2 hours) for the taught sessions. These started at 6pm and finished at 9pm. Needless to say that I had to concentrate, to fight off the urge to sleep as we had to tackle 14 topic plus a major assignment for which I obtained an A grade. I had chosen for my dissertation the impact of private healthcare on the NHS and, surprisingly for an NHS chief officer, gained access and support from private hospitals and establishments.

I also felt that I had repaid the debt by acquiring new skills and expertise which had enabled me to gain incremental promotions through the various NHS organisation which, during my time, several of the eight Secretaries of State for Health and Social Services (1970 – 88) and Secretaries of State for Health (1988 – 90) had imposed on the NHS. From Sir Keith Joseph, when I joined in 1970 to William Waldergrave when I left in 1990, most had stayed in post for only two years and during their sojourn had sought to shape the NHS in their own partisan way. Many would be quickly forgotten on leaving their post by NHS staff. The population served by the NHS was also changing quite significantly. Advances in public health meant that people were living longer and suffered from more long term treatable conditions. The original concept of one of the more memorable and longer serving Ministers of Health (there was no Secretary of State then) Aneurin Bevan– 1945- 1951), who introduced the NHS, that it would provide free health care for all, became a greater resource challenge. In seeking to resolve these issues, actions which included constantly tinkering with structures and pillorying managers on whom there was reliance to implement the changes attracted considerable publicity. Several years later the Health and Social Care Act 2012, introduced by another two year term Secretary of State, Andrew Lansley (2010-2012) continued the trend even though it was pushed through with considerable opposition from knowledgeable healthcare professional organisations and experienced healthcare individuals who saw the Act as the biggest revolution in the NHS and disguised privatisation. Only time will tell whether these judgements were correct.

Office at National Temperance Hospital –metal bars outside - 1970.

Lewisham Hospital cricket team, author standing extreme left - about to make a century (in his dreams!). C1979

Enjoying, with beard, first house in Manor Park, East London - 1973.

Dartford & Gravesham Health Authority Members with Executives - 1988 author back row standing on a chair!

Biographical information of members of Dartford and Gravesham Health Authority - 1986.

Dartford & Gravesham Health Authority – Executive Board - 1986.

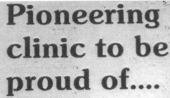

Pioneering clinic to be proud of....

The Oaks Clinic in Swanley is a reflection of Dartford and Gravesham Health Authority's commitment to the town.

By Aylin Fox
Guest reporter

▶ The Oaks Clinic.

Article in Swanley Times – announcing completion of Pioneering Clinic.

HEALTH MATTERS

Health chief leaves for job in Botswana

by Olga English

▶ Peter Ramrayka and Swanley's Oaks Health Clinic

New team out to balance bo

Health Chief leaves for job in Botswana. Article in Health Matters, Dartford Times - 1990.

142

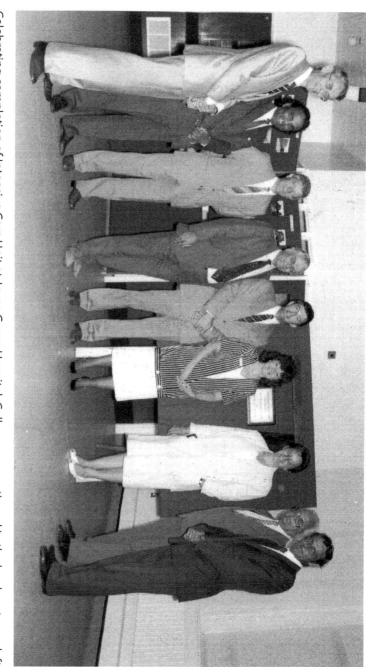

Celebrating completion of Intensive Care Unit at Joyce Green Hospital. Colleagues mentioned in the book, extreme left Tony Marchant, District General Manager next to author 4th left Tim Brinton, Chairman Dartford and Gravesham Health Authority 2nd right Dr. George Stratton former Chairman of the Authority - 1988.

Damaged Car – after major accident. 1988

God daughter Sienna with her Mum Aylia Fox.

CHAPTER 8

PAYING BACK – COMMUNITY ACTIVITIES

VOLUNTARY SERVICE - JUSTICE OF THE PEACE – MAGISTRATE

While developing my healthcare management career I have always retained a passionate interest in providing voluntary service to the community as I saw the twin track path of professional development and contributing to the community particularly satisfying.

The Chairman of the existing, sacked then reinstated Lambeth, Southwark and Lewisham Area Health Authority Teaching, was Stan Hardy, who held a George Cross and a British Empire Medal. Stan was a local Lewisham man who represented Bellingham Ward and was the London Borough of Lewisham Mayor - 1974/75. As a senior manager in Lewisham Health District I met him on several occasions and in one of our conversations he said that I had all the qualities to be a JP – a Justice of the Peace. I was flattered by this comment and filled in the necessary form.

"Peter Sahib, what is a JP?"

"Basdeo, the position is ancient, originating in 1195 under King Richard 1 when knights were appointed to ensure that the law was upheld and were known as 'King's Peace'! Over the years many changes occurred but the current role stems from the Municipal Corporations Act 1835 giving authority to the Lord Chancellor to nominate candidates with local advice for appointment to the Crown. So in England and Wales, it is a judicial appointment to sit on a bench in a magistrates' court along with two others to dispense summary justice – offences which carry up to six months in prison, to a maximum of one year of imprisonment over not less than two indictable offences. They are meant to be responsible lay people but are advised by a legally qualified 'Justices Clerk' on matters of law.

JPs are authorised to sign warrants for arrest, to search properties, witness applications for passports and other documents where specified. Senior magistrates also sit in a higher court, the Crown Court, as lay assessors with a Crown Court Judge"

"Boy, sorry I mean Peter Sahib, you were a big shot sitting on a bench dispensing justice. *Me a go back in me bottle - you continue*"

"Ok Basdeo, no more wise cracks from you or I will put a permanent cork on the bottle"!

It was a pleasant surprise when several months after speaking with Stan Hardy and thinking no more about my application, I received a letter from the Lord Chancellor's office appointing me as Justice of the Peace for Inner London, with effect from April 1981, with duties at Camberwell and Tower Bridge Magistrates' Court. My initial plan of studying to become a lawyer and hopefully a Magistrate, side tracked when I entered the Royal Air Force, had become a reality, albeit as Lay not a paid Stipendiary Magistrate. I would spend the next nine years becoming more and more involved in magisterial work. Elected to the local management body of Justices, the General Purpose Committee of the South Central Petty Session Division (as it then was) I also sat in the Inner London Crown Court, with a judge as one of the two JPs on appropriate referral cases from the Magistrates' Court. For the second time in my life I would be taking a public oath, but unlike the Royal Air Force when it was more concerned with defence of the realm this oath took the following form:

"I swear that I will well and truly serve our Sovereign Lady Queen Elizabeth the Second, in the office of Justice of the Peace and I will do right to all manner of people after the laws and usages of the Realm without fear or favour, affection or ill will"

In the nine years I spent as a magistrate, resigning in 1990 to take up a health consultancy position overseas, these words guided my behaviour on the bench and was at the front of my thoughts in my subsequent interaction at work and with my friends and colleagues.

Magisterial sittings, being part time and voluntary, took place twice a month and attendance at the Crown Court on average every two months. Sittings were supported by a raft of training which were compulsory and were invaluable as one became more experienced and had to share chairing the bench of three, with two other colleagues. The experience gained would have a lasting effect on my future paid public sector involvement and international voluntary work.

POLITICAL ACTIVITY – SOCIAL DEMOCRATIC PARTY

I have also always been interested in politics but as I became more senior in the NHS I was wary that overt political activity might be career-limiting, so kept a careful balance. The birth of the Social Democratic Party (SDP) in 1981 as a response to the perceived threats from the Trotskyist section of the Labour party resonated with me. My views went against the grain which suggested that most - if not all - immigrants especially those from the 'new' Commonwealth (i.e. those of colour) saw the Labour party as their natural home. I was not in sympathy with the Conservatives' right wing dogmatic views and felt at the time that the Liberal party did not have a broad enough appeal to be considered seriously for government. I thought that the 'gang of four' as the breakaway Labour Members of Parliament who formed the SDP were called - Roy Jenkins, David Owen, Bill Rodgers and Shirley Williams - had a real chance of making a difference as so many people were supporting them. A year and five months after the SDP was formed, I broke a private vow that I made not to formally join a political party, either in the UK or the Guyanese diaspora in London and became a member of the SDP in August, 1982.

I attended on a regular basis SDP meetings enjoying the comradeship with, amongst others, Patsy and John Grigg. John was a supporter of the Anti-Apartheid Movement with a long an interesting political career. He inherited the title of Baron Altrincham in 1955, on his father's death, but was the second person to disclaim his peerage (after Viscount Stansgate – Tony Benn, a Labour party Cabinet Minister) taking advantage of the 1963 Peerage Act. John and I and SDP activists had some lively discussions at his home in Blackheath, London, where our meetings were held. Listening to his analysis of politics at the time and his views as to what was needed to make Britain a better place to live in, confirmed to me that I had made the right choice in joining the SDP. In the following years I became more involved in political activities.

Although my employment base had changed from Lewisham to Dartford I continued to live in Lewisham and active in politics in the area. I progressed within SDP gaining a place on the approved list for Prospective Parliamentary Candidates (PPCs) and being selected as the SDP/Alliance candidate for St. Mildred's ward in Lewisham in the 1986 London Council elections. Alas, my 661 votes were not sufficient to be elected (a strong Tory ward their most successful candidate gained 2,243 votes). Although I did not pursue opportunities to start a parliamentary career (successful professional options were pulling me away) I was glad to play a small part (canvassing, delivering leaflets etc.) in the SDP candidate Rosie Barnes' astonishing win in the neighbouring Greenwich by-election in 1987 which gained massive national coverage and helped to keep the Party firmly on the political map.

THE MAGISTRATES ASSOCIATION
Coat of Arms

'Ratione et Consilio'
By reason and sound judgement.

Outside Camberwell Green Magistrates Court first sitting as a Magistrate/ Justice of the Peace - April, 1981.

Meeting Shirley Williams at Liberal democrats Conference years after SDP was formed, Now Baroness Williams of Cosby.

SDP/Alliance flyer – London Council elections 1986. SDP/Alliance new on the political scene - Mary Bright received 746 votes, 661 for me and 698 for Charles Rose. Three Conservatives elected each receiving over 2000!

CHAPTER 9

AT THE TROPIC OF CAPRICORN

BOTSWANA

With the congratulatory messages and good wishes from Dartford friends and colleagues still ringing in my ears, I left the falling leaves and mild 15C temperature of an English autumn for the searing 40C heat of Botswana.

"Peter Sahib, just… just… just… hold on a minute. What would happen to me if it is going to be so hot and I am in a bottle?"

"Don't worry, Basdeo, I will let you out, from time to time but please promise me you will not get up to any mischief, throwing things around or making strange noises. The San and Hambukushu tribes live in Botswana and they have their own spirits who might not welcome you so we have to be careful"

"Thanks, Peter Sahib, I renew my promise to be a good Bacoo. *Me na want to get involved with any African Jumbie.* It would help if you could give a brief background about Botswana"

"OK Basdeo, I am glad that you do not wish to be involved with African spirits, I will continue".

Botswana was a former British protectorate called Bechuanaland. It became independent in 1966, the same year as Guiana. It had an African Royal family and one of their kings (*Kgosi)* who inherited the title when he was only four years old, married in 1947 a white British woman, Ruth Williams, a former Women Auxiliary Air Force ambulance driver and clerk at Lloyd's in London who was born in Blackheath (where years later I came to live). This caused tremendous upset both in Botswana (where the chiefs of Khama's tribe wanted the marriage to be annulled) and in neighbouring Apartheid South Africa, immersed in racial discriminatory laws and practices, where inter- racial marriages were banned. The British government which at the time wanted to retain good relations with South Africa, succumbed to pressure and exiled Khama and his wife in 1951, only allowing them to return as private citizens five years later. Khama went on to become Prime Minister then President when his country became independent. He was also knighted by the Queen.

"Peter Sahib, that was funny don't you think- a King gaining knighthood from a Queen?"

"Yes Basdeo, very observant, but I will continue."

Sir Seretse, as he now became, remained in post for 14 years transforming the country from one of the poorest in Africa to one of the most stable and, with one of the fastest growing economies in the world, the richest in sub Saharan Africa, if not of Africa as a whole. The Pula, the local currency, was considered to be one of the strongest in the world.

With this history of fighting off Apartheid-South Africa, with its decades of racial discriminatory laws, I wondered what effect it would have on Botswana as my new position was to lead a team of three other British consultants – a nurse, an engineer and a bio-medical devices technician, all of whom were white, as we sought to support the Batswana (citizens of Botswana) staff in developing Princess Marina Hospital(PMH) in the capital, Gaborone, from a general hospital into a national referral hospital, in particular serving the southern part of the country.

I need not have worried as there was no obvious racial tension in the country and we quickly integrated with our local colleagues. The project team for the building was led by an architect from Singapore of Chinese extraction and the rest of the construction staff was a mini United Nations with people of many creeds and colours including white South Africans.

The appointment came with a contractual promise of a house which took nearly six months to materialise. To compensate for this we were accommodated, with all meals provided free as part of the contract, at the Gaborone Sun, a five star hotel in the capital, ten minutes' walk from the hospital. Our waistlines gradually grew as we enjoyed the lavish three meals a day international dishes. We put off the recommended daily 10,000 steps exercise with the excuse that we were not accustomed to the heat which in the dry winter season (May to October) – the temperature ranged from 28C/80F to a 38C/100F and in the wet summer season (November to April) from 20C/69F to 32C/87F Suggestions that, in common with other countries bordering the Sahara, we should take advantage of the significantly cooler mornings and evenings were met with equally lamentable excuses.

As the principal consultant and leader of the team my immediate task was to establish effective working relationships with key stakeholders – Dr. Eddie Maganau, Permanent Secretary at the Ministry of Health, Dr. Dudu Mahloane, Medical Superintendent at PMH, and Dr. Bright Bagwasi, Senior Consultant Surgeon. Their willingness to collaborate, their humility and eagerness to learn (not to mention genuine friendship) made the work a pleasure. After many hours of developing new models of clinical operational policies and procedures and programme management discussions, Dudu, Bright and I would relax at the end of the day with a cool beer or two to put the world to rights. Bright, a generous host, would suggest out- of-town visits to places of particular national interest such as Mahalapye located on the imaginary line of latitude which encircles the earth separating the Southern Hemisphere (the Tropic of Capricorn) from the Northern Hemisphere (Tropic of Cancer) There is a small monument just outside of Mahalapye to mark this geographic feature and you can stand on the line painted to mark the spot with one foot in the Tropic of Capricorn and the other in the Tropic of Cancer!.

As British consultants we were accorded the special privilege of being invited to the Presidential State House for Independence Day celebrations and had the pleasure of meeting the relatives of Sir Seretse Khama. The successful completion of the Princess Marina Hospital development and a visit from the Minister of Health, brought much satisfaction to the Batswana people, members of my team, and the community served by the new facility.

"Peter Sahib, whilst I have been sweating in this bottle, I have been trying to ask you what have you learnt from this experience?"

"Well Basdeo, I recognised the importance of adapting British models to suit local conditions, being an enabler to give locals the expertise and tools to do the jobs themselves. Respect, especially for elders and the unusual mannerisms of Batswana women when first greeting you. The process includes a slight bending of the right knee, a handshake with the right hand outstretched and left arm placed on it and a lovely welcome phrase of "Dumela Mma, Dumela Rraa." (welcome madam, welcome sir). Such warmth is conveyed by this action. Then there is the general guidance that you have to be careful when meeting an individual for the first time and saying "how are you?" You need to be prepared to allow time to hear a detailed response giving information from the time the person got up in the morning to the time of meeting you – the details of journey could be very long! One other interesting observation Basdeo was the system of *Kgotla, a* decision making community meeting , chaired by a village chief, in which a person is allowed to speak uninterrupted, is listened to by all and a decision is reached by the Chief and respected by all present. Perhaps a lesson here for those of us involved in general management and leadership."

"Thank you Peter Sahib, please continue."

There was also road trips to many interesting surrounding areas with my two wheel drive Toyota Carina which I had shipped from England. One was on a visit with my daughters to Chobe National Park when, trying to explore areas off the main road, we became stuck in the mud with the wheels of the car going round and round but not moving. With not a soul in sight, and no means of communication we feared we would be fried in the heat of the day or frozen to death by the cold at night. As I was most concerned about the welfare of my two young daughters and, as the situation was becoming somewhat fraught, a "knight in shining armour" in the person of a Motswana (an individual citizen of Botswana) on a tractor, came literally out of nowhere and pulled us out. His name was Obiajulu. He refused to accept any payment for his help, gave us strong handshakes and waved us on to our next destination,

Victoria Falls (known to the locals as Mosi-oa Tunya Toakaleya Tonga – the Smoke that thunders!) in Zimbabwe.

The roar of the falls could be heard from 24 miles (40km) away and the spray and mist rising from the falling water could be seen from about the same distance. It's 5,604 feet (1,708 metres) wide and 354 feet (108metres) high - quite a sight to behold. I was impressed at the wide range of tourist facilities which had been created around it and, as someone born in Guyana, I wondered why Kaiteur Falls in the country, which at 370 feet (113 metres) wide and 741 feet (226 metres) high, the 10th highest waterfall in the world, twice the height of Victoria, had not attracted a similar type of international tourist interest. A task here for Guyana's tourist industry!

Travelling by road from Botswana to Zimbabwe we saw some of the stark economic differences between the two countries. The shops in the rural areas were sparse and basic with none of the plentiful supplies of food found in Botswana. The people were, by and large, fairly friendly but one sensed that they were not happy with their lot.

I also made over-ground trips to Natal and Johannesburg in South Africa which were pleasant, roads fairly good and having just come out of the dreadful clutches of Apartheid, the racially discriminatory signs were still up in some places but my reception, as a person of colour, in hotels and other leisure places indicated that the barriers were down, at least for visitors.

Natal was particularly interesting as there was much evidence of the British Raj instigated Indian migration, including a scattering of conspicuous well decorated Hindu temples and Muslim mosques, if rather incongruously placed near to western type buildings. Gandhiji would have been proud to know that the seeds he had sown all those years ago when he started his Satyagraha movement in 1903, had blossomed and his people had survived and prospered.

In 1992, when I left Botswana, the life expectancy at birth was 64.08 years for women and 58.95 for men. I was very saddened to learn that by 2004 it had dropped to 47.64 for women and 46.69 for men largely due to the AIDS epidemic which had swept sub Saharan Africa. However by 2013 the World Health

Organisation suggested that it had risen to 63 for women and 61 for men. It was hoped that that the rise would be maintained as AIDS/HIV treatment continued to improve. Princess Marina Hospital had become a major centre for the treatment of the disease. I hoped that the ground work which we had carried out in developing the hospital into a national referral centre and mentoring Batswana in clinical practices and general management, played a small part in supporting the health and welfare of the colleagues we had left behind.

My memories of the happy times in Botswana have been captured and re-recreated with much humour, in the series of novels by Scottish author, Alexander McCall, called No1 Ladies' Detectives Agency. Mma Precious Ramotswe, the central character of the books, brings alive many of the Batswana I had met.

Laying foundations for development of extension to Princess Marina Hospital - Botswana - developing a National Referral Hospital for the southern part of the country - 1990.

Office in Princess Marina with poster of Botswana Cabinet in background 1990.

Gaborone Sun Hotel – Botswana, room and full board for several months whilst waiting for accommodation to be provided - 1990.

In front of government building – Pretoria – South Africa, pleasant visit with no overt discriminatory experiences (some Apartheid signs were still seen but ignored!) - 1991.

CHAPTER 10

WORKING WITH THE DIASPORA

BACK IN BLIGHTY

Returning to the UK, and my hometown London, meant a readjustment to working life.

The changes in the NHS which had been started when I left were now in full swing. The view of the then Regional General Manager (RGM), that re-entry at a top level would be relatively easy as I now had international consultancy experience working at both hospital operational and at strategic Ministry of Health levels, had changed. The RGM had moved on and most senior positions were comfortably filled at least for the short term.

As the bug of consultancy had also bitten me, with the freedom to act and the pleasure of giving advice without the worry of line management, some would say, mischievously, borrowing organisations' watches to tell them to the time, meant that there were other openings to explore. GP fundholding, introduced in 1991 to give general practitioners budgetary responsibilities as part of the NHS internal market, needed support and following a conversation with one of my former Dartford and Gravesham Board colleagues, the GP representative on the Board, Dr. Tony Crick, a period of giving advice and support to a group of Kent GPs started. Relatively short term consultancies suited me fine as I could also restart my voluntary work in the community.

INDO-CARIBBEAN CULTURAL ASSOCIATION (ICCA)/INDO CARIBBEAN ORGANISATION

Indo- Caribbeans (mostly from Guyana and Trinidad) and their descendants in the UK are estimated to be around 50,000 + (precise number is hard to come by as UK census forms do not list them as a separate group, no doubt because people have to tick the box on the form as 'Asian other'). Consequently, there was sparse knowledge of the group amongst the general UK community, and in particular local authority policy makers in Greater London area where most of Indo- Caribbean people live. Unlike other immigrant groups Indo- Caribbeans have not concentrated in any specific area but are dispersed across the capital and therefore access as a group to public funds to support cultural activities, services for the elderly in particular dietary and health needs were not as effective as it could be. The special characteristics of Indo Caribbeans people include their strong Indian cultural identity – heritage, food, music, and dance - English speaking but also having Caribbean cultural background. These tended to set them apart from their brothers and sisters from the Indian sub-continent in the UK. Although as would be expected, there is kinship and mutual co-operation between the groups.

As the first generation of Indo-Caribbean people who emigrated to the UK from the late 50s were getting older and, as the majority live in the Greater London area, there was a desire to promote and celebrate our cultural heritage and to share these with the indigenous population and other immigrant groups. It was also felt that regular events and meetings, in a non - religious setting, would enable us to identify particular needs of the community and where required and necessary to make those needs known to official bodies.

Prior to going abroad I had become involved with Indo-Caribbean Cultural Association, (ICCA) , a non- religious charity set up to foster good community relations by promoting social events and in particular to showcase Indo–Caribbean culture. These became extremely popular with the target communities, especially the occasional Saturday night socials. ICCA ran successfully for several years, had the backing of all sections of the Indo-Caribbean diaspora (especially those from Trinidad and Guyana) and, importantly for us, the support of Arif Ali, a well-known publisher and brilliant champion for bringing the races together, who gave us free advertisements in his influential newspapers – *Caribbean Times and Asian Times*. Unfortunately, in the absence of some of the founding leaders who had moved away or, in my case moved abroad on consultancy assignments, ICCA was taken over by others, who might not have shared our vision, and it eventually folded. Knowledge of this left me rather disappointed and to resurrect the spirit of ICCA the Indo-Caribbean Organisation was set up, again with Arif's support and continues to thrive, albeit not to the same level of activity. Our ambition was (and is) to have greater involvement with younger people.

We were very fortunate to have someone of Arif's standing in the community supporting us and we were all extremely pleased when the European Union declared 1997 as the European Year Against Racism and Arif was awarded the European Year Against Racism Champion (Individual) Gold Standard Award.

GUYANA MEDICAL RELIEF COMMITTEE/ GUYHEALTH (UK)

In Guyana, after years of dubious elections, a new fully democratically elected government came into power in 1992. The need to get all the support possible to rebuild the country was brought into sharp focus by an outbreak of cholera. The then Guyanese Minister of Health, Gail Texeira, visited and the diaspora were called upon to provide a helping hand. With other colleagues, one of whom was Laleshwar Singh who would eventually become Guyana's High Commissioner to the UK, we formed the Guyana Medical Relief Committee (GMRC). Working for a short time with this group, most of whom were from an Indo Guyanese background, it became apparent to me that the perception of one race, Indians, providing support to what some perceived as an Indian led government, would only perpetuate in the UK a situation which unfortunately existed in Guyana prior to the new government taking power (i.e. Afro Guyanese supporting an Afro- Guyanese led government)

Using the relationship which had been formed in the GMRC, I asked the High Commissioner for permission to use the Commission's premises as a venue for an event and set about inviting most , if not all, Guyanese organisations in London and various parts of the UK. The response was overwhelming. At the function there were Guyanese of all races, representatives from the government in power (the Peoples Progressive Party) and the opposition (Peoples National Congress), Christians, Hindus and Muslims other groups of the Guyanese diaspora. The event, hosted by the High Commissioner, was truly memorable and hailed in the Guyanese community in the UK as a model to follow. The Association of Guyanese Nurses and Allied Profession (AGNAP) was one of our founding members and in one of their celebratory booklets a reflective summary of our launch was given prominence including the full list of those who had attended.

As the elected Chairman of the group I was pleased that we had played some part in demonstrating unity in our adopted country which we hoped would send positive messages to the people in the country of our birth.

In subsequent years, as a registered UK charity, GUYHEALTH(UK) continued to support Guyana's health services through organising the collection and shipping of surplus hospital equipment, organising visits to health establishments in the UK for Guyanese personnel and generally be an organisation available to provide help and support when needed.

GUYHEALTH (UK)
A history of cooperation – and an example that went unheeded!

H.E. the High Commissioner for Guyana with committee members at the launch of GUYHEALTH (UK)

AGNAP(UK) can indeed be proud that so many of its members took a founding part in Guyhealth (UK).

In 1992 there was a landmark election in Guyana, and a peaceful transition of government from PNC to PPP. In the U.K., Lalweshwar KN Singh CCH was appointed the new High Commissioner for Guyana.

The brainfathers of Guyhealth, Lal Singh and Peter Ramrayka, had only recently formed the Guyana Medical Relief Committee, of which Lal could not now remain a member. The solution was to convert the Committee to the present Guyana Healthcare Coordinating Group, with His Excellency as Patron. He put out a call to ALL Guyanese in the UK to participate, either in a corporate or individual capacity, and the response was remarkable and – fifteen years on – still a lesson to us all.

At the launch of Guyhealth UK in 1993, we put aside race, party politics, religion, gender and agenda, and we all sat around the High Commissioner's table with one heart, a love of Guyana and concern for the health and welfare of our friends and families back home.

Berbice sat with Demerara; PPP with PNC; Muslim, Hindu and Christian sat together; all six peoples of Guyana were there, man and woman, young and old. We met, we discussed, we fund-raised and we socialized. Yes, there were a few healthy differences of opinion, but no serious rifts, no walkouts. We were there for a purpose, not to massage vanities or to pursue private goals. And we succeeded. Our success was not only the material aid that we sent to our country. Our major success, an example which passed largely unnoticed, was that in this microcosm of Guyana in London we were able to work together without rancour, rivalry or loss of respect for one another.

Just look at some of the participating organizations: The Caribbean Hindu Society, the Caribbean Islamic Cultural Society, the Indo-Caribbean Cultural Association, the Guyana Berbice Association, the West Demerara Reunion Club, the PPP, the PNC, the World Union of Guyanese, the Queen's College of Guyana Association, Friends of Guyana, the Caribbean Indian Women's League, the Dr CC Nicholson Foundation and, of course, AGNAP.

Individuals, and representatives of the above and other organizations, included Peter (chair), Dr Eddie Adams & Ian Wishart (vicechairmen), Lyn Richards & Fazia Ouhla (secretaries), Inez Corbin (treasurer) Olston Beresford, Glen Greaves, Raymond Kudrath, Alma Patrick, Mike Saywack, Dr Frank Williams, Jim Jhinkoo, Beryl Curtis, Gloria Hector, Thelma Lewis, Harry Persaud, Maurice Persaud, Carmen Singh, Betty & John Why, Dr Albert Fortune, Dr Kalam Khan-Karamat, Louis Park, Patsy Fagan, Cynthia Richards, Von Cadogan, Faiyaz Alli, Janet François, Mohammed Kayyam., Bruce Nobrega, Chris Chunnilall, Lee Samuels, Sydney Marshall, Rebecca Vaughan. Associated celebrities included: Bernie Grant, Ram John Holder, Jessica & Eric Huntley, Margaret Brayton, Clive

Launch of Guyhealth(UK) *(Article from Association of Guyanese Nurses & Allied Professions 20th Anniversary brochure (acknowledged).*

With Dr, Behri Ramsarran – Guyana's Minister of Health – Georgetown - discussing how Guyhealth(UK) could be of assistance and taking away 3 top priority needs - 2013.

Launch of Indo- Caribbean Cultural Organisation (ICO) founding members include From left back row Ashwini Ganpat, Suresh Rambaran, Terry Khan, author, Ali Mohammed, Hardeo Gopie, Anjanie Narayan-Dookie, Fidel Persaud Front: Shirley Ramnarine and Susan Bharath - 2002.

With Arif Ali – friend and tremendous supporter of Indo- Caribbean Cultural Association and Indo - Caribbean Organisation.

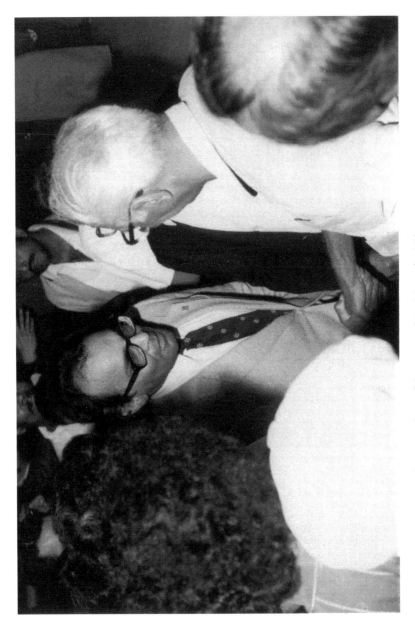

Meeting Dr. Cheddi Jagan, late President of Guyana on his visit to the UK.

Social function in London – with President Bharat Jagdeo of Guyana.

Guyhealth(UK) arranged visit to Southwest London and St. George's Mental Health trust. L to R. H.E. Laleshwar Singh, Guyana's High Commissioner, author, Dr. Nigel Fisher, Chief Executive, SWLTG, Hon. Dr. Leslie Ramsammy, Minister of Health, Jan Hildreth, Chairman – SWLTG.

Kaiteur Falls – Guyana.

Photo opportunity at Kaiteur Falls.

With Dr. Leslie Ramsammy (L) Guyana Minister of Health and Michael Khan (C) CEO, Georgetown Public Hospital Corporation, being shown around the hospital and discussing how Guyhealth(UK) could continue with its support.

Committee members and supporters at the launch of Guyhealth(UK) with Guyana's High Commissioner (centre front row). Author (back row with bow tie) - 1993.

Disused Berbice (Mental) Hospital.

New mental health facilities – Berbice National Psychiatric Hospital.

With Dr. Vishwa Mahadeo, Chief Executive, Berbice Regional Health Authority met to discuss Guyhealth(UK)'s continuing aid in particular regarding Mental Health services – 2013.

CHAPTER 11

INTERNATIONAL CONSULTANCIES

AMONGST THE BELIEVERS - PAKISTAN

Foreign adventure loomed again as I was recruited by the Nuffield Institute of Health at Leeds University to be part of their team on the second family health project in Pakistan. I was engaged as the Management Systems Development Consultant Adviser in-country as well as a Lecturer in Healthcare Management at Leeds University, working in liaison with the British Council in Lahore. This was because the funding was in part through the UK's Department for International Development.

The project was the US$48 million Second Family Health Project covering Punjab, Baluchistan and the Federal Ministry of Health. The main objective was to improve the health status of the population of the two provinces. This was to be achieved through assisting with the implementation of the provincial development programme, concentrating on Primary Health, Preventive and Promotive Services, Strengthening Primary Health services from the Village to District level, Staff Development and Management and Organisational Development.

My job was to carry out organisation and management review of the health services in Punjab (the largest province in Pakistan with more than 60 million people), recommend and implement new organisational structures, develop provincial and district healthcare training institutes, identify Pakistan senior health managers (nearly all clinical doctors) and recommend them for training at the Nuffield Institute in Leeds. Also with the appointment was a requirement to work with colleagues to introduce strategic health planning in all four provinces attending their capitals – Punjab (Lahore), Sindh

(Karachi), Khyber Pakhtunkhwa (Peshawar) Balochistan (Quetta), the disputed area of Azad Kashmir (Muzaffarabad) and the Ministry of Health in the capital Islamabad. I regularly travelled by air and road to their capitals.

Arriving in Lahore on 1st January 1995, was a momentous occasion for me, as it would be the first time in my life that I would reside in a country where I was not seen as a minority due to my skin colouring. Any thought that my Hindu surname would be quickly recognised and a barrier in this staunchly Muslim state was promptly set aside as I was given an extremely warm welcome by the people that I had come to guide and develop and also hopefully learn from. I was indeed regarded with great respect and referred to with the courtesy title Peter Sahib (the form of address Basdeo is using!)

The relative cushy life of an expatriate (and a British one in particular) was evident in being provided, as part of the contract, with a bungalow in the up-market sought after district of Gulberg. In common with other expatriates I was engaged at the going rate for the expertise I had to offer which made it possible for me to engage local staff. I had three servants. They were a cook, a gardener and a watchman who ensured that I lived well. Daily sumptuous meals did nothing for my waistline. A Land Rover with a driver was provided to take me to and from work daily. The joy of moving around the country racially inconspicuous was for me something to be treasured. My strategic planning consultancy involved working closely with the Ministries of Health in all four provinces. At each, after a working sessions lasting from two to four days, with senior healthcare colleagues, I was entertained with elaborate meals or taken out on tours to historical places of interest. Two of these were near to Harappa in Punjab and Mohenjo-Daro in Sindh, part of the Indus Valley Civilisation (3300-1300 BC). As someone of Indian ancestry visiting the sites of one of the three earliest civilisation in the old world (the other two being Ancient Egypt and Mesopotamia) made me feel very proud. However, I couldn't help thinking that in my school days more of this incredible heritage should have been taught to me and my peers.

Official trips to Muzaffarabad in Azad (Free) Kashmir (the other Indian part known as Jammu and Kashmir) and to Quetta in Balochistan were particularly exciting as both were regarded as politically sensitive areas but of course nothing like what they are now, in particular Quetta and Peshawar, both on the borders of Afghanistan and deeply involved in the ongoing war.

As a non-Muslim in an overwhelming Islamic country - but being of the same race and colour as the majority of citizens - caused embarrassment from time to time. On one occasion travelling on Pakistan's airline during Ramadan, the Muslim month of fasting in daylight hours, was particularly tricky. Sitting next to serious looking heavily bearded travelling companion fingering prayer beads, I was faced with the dilemma of either foregoing the on-board meal when offered by the cabin staff and keeping my identity and the companionship secure, or accepting the meal and being singled out as a foreigner. I opted for the former!

Respecting my colleagues' beliefs during Ramadan meant that I also refrained from eating in public places and in my office. Local staff were regularly dropping in for advice or just to have a chat. My admiration of the discipline exercised by colleagues in refraining from fasting was coupled with astonishment at the elaborate evening meals which were laid on to break the fast at sunset. Called Iftar, Arabic for break fast, it is a happy occasion and I had the pleasure of being invited to several colleagues' homes to experience the ritual.

Regular hospitality from hosts during my stay encouraged me to reciprocate, which I was pleased to do. It was here that my trusted cook, Nathaniel, came in very handy. He prepared delicious Pakistani dishes and my home became open house every Friday and Saturday (the Muslim weekend) to a string of visitors both local and expatriate. Alcohol, which as an expatriate I could purchase from one of the five star hotels using the special permit which I had obtained from the Local Authority, was freely available. But I needed to be careful in ensuring that those who were not allowed to, did not partake. This was a delicate task but my guests always respected the constraints, at least I am sure that they did when I left the room!

Collecting the alcohol from the hotel was also a task that I needed to handle carefully. The collection point was at the side of the building which had a separate entrance and the local police kept an observant eye on the 'comings and goings'. As I looked like a local, I was occasionally stopped. Offers to let me go on the payment of a 'fine' were firmly rejected on the production of my alcohol permit. Word soon got around that I was a British Sahib, so there was no point trying to get rupees from me!

In Lahore we worked well with other international consultants and one in particular Jacinthe Desmarais, a French Canadian woman who was particularly interested in everything British, appreciated the work we were doing with the health services in the province. She looked for opportunities for greater collaboration especially in synchronising health promotion and gender equality messages. We in turn admired her tenacity and her desire to make a difference, particularly as she was a foreign woman working with an overwhelmingly male dominated professional group. Many enjoyable work sessions were spent with her trying to find ways to resolve common challenges. As a Management Consultant working closely with Punjab's Ministry of Health, I received many glowing reports from senior Ministry officials about the positive impact Jacinthe was making.

The local staff at the headquarters of the consultancy in Mozang Road in Lahore was, in common with British establishments in Pakistan, a good mixture of male and female, Muslims and Christians and as far as possible other tribal groups. So we had a Pathan as one of our chief negotiators when minor local operational issues needed to be resolved, Punjabis as drivers and clerks and Christian typists. Strong team spirit developed between the British consultants and the staff and I was particularly fortunate in being given that little bit of extra warmth, I felt, because of my racial background.

I was particularly keen to learn Urdu, which is closely related to Hindi (the language of my forefathers) but different in the written form as it follows a Persian script with many words borrowed from Persian and Arabic whilst Hindi uses a Devanagari script.

My language gurus were many of the junior doctors I was providing consultancy to –Dr. Saquib Mehmood Choudhri (my 'Chota Bhai' (little brother) and Dr. Imtiaz being the two most prominent. One of our support staff, Mumtaz, was also particularly helpful. She had studied at a British University and was fluent in English. Our long consultancy journeys to districts outside of Lahore - Multan, Islamabad and Murree - were opportunities for her to check my Urdu knowledge and pronunciations and for me to impart my professional knowledge and experience. We shared a fascination with Pakistani/ Indian music in particular two Hindi songs current at the time- *Ek Ladki Ko Dekha* (when I saw this girl) *and Aaja Nachle,* (come, let's dance) which I had purchased from a bazaar in Gulberg. Both were lead songs from popular Hindi films (and titles by the same names). The leading actress from *Aaja Nachle,* Madhuri Dixit was widely admired in Lahore (and no doubt elsewhere in Pakistan) as were many other Indian films, film stars and Hindi songs.

Strange as it might appear from media coverage, although there are serious disagreements between the two countries, amongst ordinary Pakistanis and Indians there is admiration for each other, especially regarding films, songs and cricket. In my view there is a significant amount of regret that tensions continue to exist, even to the present day, when if they were to build on the strong cultural connections, the region could be more prosperous and large sections of their populations would be lifted out of poverty.

Of the various tasks, the Provisional Health Development Centre (PHDC) was a significant challenge, as we needed to develop a major teaching centre along with District Health Development Centres for the province from scratch. We were ably assisted in addressing this by two extremely competent Directors. Dr.Anwar Bughvi laid the groundwork which was excellently developed by Dr.Darakshan Badar a female clinician and leader. As a woman in a male dominated environment she showed the professionalism and can-do spirit which were required to promote a new initiative and inculcate a sense of ownership amongst all those involved. The PHDC was successfully launched, as were a number of DHDCs in districts throughout Punjab with District Health Officers in place. In Lodhran (Dr. Samee Ullah Sheikh), Okara (Capt. Dr. Mukhtar Ali), Sialkot (Dr. Syed Talat Iqbal), Sheikhpura (Dr. Mohammed Safdar), Rahim Yar Khan (Dr. Fazal Mehmood) and Rawalpindi Dr. Fayyaz Ahmad Ranjha). We supported these colleagues in the formation of new ways of working and felt sure that in time they would become the future leaders of healthcare in Pakistan (hence naming them!).

We were also successful in developing and implementing plans to devolve management responsibilities from the centre in Lahore to districts by creating District Health Authorities (DHAs) and setting up District Management Teams (DMT). Modelled on the 1974 structure of the NHS, but with specific adaptations to suit Pakistani societal and health management cultures, they were very much welcomed. In consultation with local people we drew up Terms of Reference for each DMT and covered a wide range of operational and strategic issues including the preparation of an Annual District Health Plan. Developing a Gender Strategy to encourage and support female workers was a key element.

The launch of the first District Health Authority was done with much fanfare. It took place in Jhelum District, in the Zilla Council Rest House. Mr. Ismail Quershi, Punjab's Provincial Secretary, Health, attending specifically to inaugurate the meeting said:

"I am delighted to be present on this historic occasion, to be part of the major health sector reform process, decentralising health care services to grass roots level. An initiative of this magnitude requires the active involvement of both the providers and recipients of the services. The membership of the Health Authority reflects that diversity and the health department look forward to cooperation of all sections of the community, private and public sectors, in ensuring that local needs are assessed and met locally and the community are truly involved in resolution of their health problems". Nawabzada Syed Shams Haider, Member of Punjab's Provincial Assembly and Chairman of the new Health Authority added that he was honoured to be invited by the Chief Minister to lead such an important organisation that was charged with the task of breaking new ground and also fulfilling the Government's mandate of making the services more accountable to local people.

To hear these significant commitments and to be congratulated on my achievements in bringing this part of the overall Second Family Health project to a very important point, was most satisfying. Throughout these major strategic and operational developments, Dr. Darakshan Badar worked closely with us, not only providing leadership but also advising us of local cultural issues which were important if we were to gain ownership and commitment to our implementation plans. It was a pleasure to be her mentor and I was delighted when, 26 years later she contacted me on a visit to London, again through the internet and I was able to welcome her and her husband for an 'English Afternoon Tea' and a catch up. This was another example of enduring friendships which are formed when working with people to build a better world, irrespective of country, nationality, race or religion.

I could not leave Pakistan without visiting the country of my forefathers – India! As Lahore was only 14 miles (22km) miles from the official road border crossing at Wagah and 20 miles (32 km) from Amritsar, the Sikhs' holy city in the Punjab, I used this route to enter the country. The welcome I received from the Sikh immigration officer was absolutely delightful. Having found out that I was a descendant of one of his ancestors who had been sent by the British Raj to build another country, I was addressed as Bhai (brother) and given a bear hug if a little prickly with his beard against my clean shaven face. Overcome with emotion I wanted to do as Pope John Paul 11 did when, on becoming Pope, he visited Warsaw in Poland in June 1979 and kissed the ground the country of his birth (and started a trend) Alas, the security situation did not make this gesture very suitable.

Harmandir Sahib (The Golden Temple) at Amritsar was a sight to behold. The English translation of the temple's name, 'The Abode of God', was built by the fourth Sikh guru, Guru Ramdaas Sahib Ji, in the 16th century (started 1585 completed 1604) and although I am not a Sikh, I felt a divine presence on entering the building by one of its four entrances (an original building structural expression of the Sikhs openness to all religions). Listening to the continuous reading of the Sikh's holy book, the Guru Grant Sahib, enjoying a meal of roti and dhal from one of the largest free kitchens in the world, serving 100,000 meals daily to all comers and taking in the atmosphere, were unique experiences I will always cherish. Visiting Harmandir Sahib obviously whetted my appetite to explore other parts of India, this most exciting and vibrant country. The 'golden triangle' of New Delhi, Agra (the Taj Mahal) and Jaipur with its Hawa Mahal (Wind Palace), an ornate five storey facade structure (with nothing behind it!) beckoned.

I was pleased that there was a direct flight from Lahore to Delhi despite the tensions between Pakistan and India and took the opportunity of visiting during Republic Day celebrations in January 1997. As a descendant of someone born in India (my grandmother) the Indian High Commission in London had given me a special visa allowing me to enter the country on multiple occasions for a period of five years from January 1996. I could stay for up to 6 months on each occasion. I intended to make maximum use of this privilege. Arriving in Delhi on their winter day was pleasantly warm for me as it was 70F (21C). The sight and sounds of this great city did not come as a total surprise as I had become accustomed to the frantic nature of travel in Pakistani cities. After booking into a hotel I headed for Raj Ghat, the memorial marking the spot where Mahatma Gandhi was cremated - Antyesti (Antim Sanskar), to pay homage to one of my great heroes. As I removed my shoes to enter, I reflected on the emotions which would have been present when Gandhiji was assassinated on 31st January 1948 and cremated on this very site the next day. Humbled but inspired, this set the scene for visiting many of the historical and tourist places in India's capital. From the Red Fort, a reminder of the power of the Mughal emperors who once ruled the country, to Coronation Park, the venue of Delhi Durbar in 1877 when Queen Victoria was proclaimed Empress of India.

Seeing these historical sites led me to India Gate, a memorial to the 82,000 Indian soldiers who died in the First World War and in the third Anglo-Afghan war in 1919. Another truly humbling and inspiring moment. Of the other fascinating places to visit in Delhi I was most impressed with the Laxminarayan Temple (Birla Temple) dedicated to the Hindu deity of that name, which was inaugurated in 1939 by Gandhiji who asked that the temple should not be restricted to Hindus of a certain caste but open to all including non-Hindus.

Saturated with the history and culture of Delhi, next stop was the 157 Miles (253km) to Agra, home of the Taj Mahal. I had seen still and motion pictures and read so much of this world heritage site that I wondered whether it would live up to my expectations. I need not have worried. It is truly magnificent. To see its beauty and grasp that it was built more than 350 years ago when none of the modern construction tools were available was mind boggling. The sadness was that it was built by the Mughal Emperor Shah Jahan as a physical structural love expression in memory of his third wife Mumtaz. Tragically his life ended in misery when his son, Aurangzeb, deposed and put him under house arrest in nearby Agra Fort, gazing at the building he had created only to be buried there. What perfidy!

The obligatory 'Princess Diana lonely posed' photograph taken (with the Taj in the background), it was time to move on to the third leg of the golden triangle, Jaipur in Rajasthan. This is a flamboyant north Indian state called the Pink City because of the colour of the stones used to construct the many impressive buildings. Other places were also painted in pink to welcome Edward, the then Prince of Wales (the title accorded to the 'Crown Prince' and future Kings of England), during his visit in 1876. Avenues in the city continue to be painted in pink giving Jaipur a most impressive appearance.

One of the most fascinating places in and around Jaipur is Hawa Mahal (Palace of Winds or Palace of the Breeze) completed in 1799. This was not a Mughal structure but proudly indigenous Rajput architecture. It was built on the orders of Maharajah Sawai Pratap Singh so that women from the royal household could see the goings on in the streets below without being seen. An intricate screen of 953 small windows designed in the form of a crown of Krishna, the Godhead of the Hindu Trinity of Deities – the Supreme

Person. Jaipur is one of the main tourist sites in India where Hindu architecture predominates as the city was developed according to Vedic planning for the comfort and prosperity of the citizens. This was due to the vision of a Bengali Brahmin architect, Vidyadhar Bhattacharya, who started work in 1727 and to whom the city was most grateful.

After a wonderful spiritual and cultural experience in the Motherland I returned to Lahore. I had been there nearly three years and the fixed term contract had come to an end. It was time to pack my bags, say my good byes (Khuda Hafiz in Urdu) and make my way back to Blighty

GIVING SIGHT TO THE DEVELOPING WORLD

FLYING TEACHING EYE HOSPITAL

As soon as I settled into my London home another international healthcare opportunity arose. I was recruited as the Mission Director of a Flying Teaching Eye Hospital. This short term assignment involved leading a team of specifically chosen international healthcare professionals and supporting aircraft ground crew to fly around the developing world providing eye surgery to those in need. In the country we visited significant sections of the population had cataracts and could go blind in the absence of timely clinical intervention. The surgery involved reversing the process and enabling them to see properly.

The work also included teaching local clinical staff on the plane through videoing the operations whilst they were taking place, in a part of the plane which was converted into an operating theatre, and concurrently giving lectures to clinical staff who would be seated in another area of the plane to see the video. The process allowed for live communication between the professionals in the operating theatre and the classroom. When the several days sessions were completed the plane would revert to normal passenger mode to fly to the next destination.

My stint took me to Varna, Bulgaria; Dhaka, Bangladesh; Khartoum, Sudan; Amman, Jordan and Ulan Bator, Mongolia.

There were also administrative /training sessions in Hong Kong, New York and Seattle. The programme involved an advance crew visiting the next country on the schedule to organise logistics, accommodation, transportation, visa and siting of the plane in a cordoned off area of the airport. We would work with the Ministry of Health and/or other concerned organisations to identify the patients who needed the operation and the health professionals who would learn from us.

Carrying out medical procedures in an operating theatre on a plane, whilst at same time teaching local doctors in an adjoining area, was innovative and it attracted considerable local interest in the countries visited. Consequently invitations were extended to (and accepted) by Presidents, Prime Ministers, Ministers of Health, a Prince of a Royal family, other top government officials, local health community and other interested groups.

As Mission Director I had the pleasure of welcoming all the VIPs who arrived in their limousines (flying their country's flag) on the controlled part of the airport where the plane was parked. I introduced them to the staff and showed them around the facilities on the aircraft. All the visitors were engaging but an abiding memory was greeting the President of Sudan, Omar Hassan Ahmad al- Bashir, dressed in his national robe. He was pleasant, spoke quietly and asked me and members of the crew several very searching questions. To read several years later that this charming man was the first sitting president to be indicted for crimes against humanity by the International Criminal Court, came as a shock. Further developments are awaited (2015) with interest.

One of the joys of providing health services in the developing world is the tremendous appreciation shown by the individual recipients and their communities. In all of the countries visited, the 'thank yous' were heart-warming and humbling, mindful of the economic situation of the societies at large. In Sudan an elaborate feast was laid on for us supplemented by songs and a peculiar dance in which people springed and swayed from one foot to the other in national costume (movements rather like a car large wiper blades in motion!).It was most enchanting.

In Mongolia the chief doctor that we were liaising with organised an event in a tent- like structure used for centuries by nomads of central Asia called a yert or ger. The atmosphere inside was mesmerising as we were showed the best of Mongolian culture. I was intrigued to find within the ger a picture of a Hindu god which I subsequently understood to have been a spin off from Buddhism which had been prevalent in the country. The Mongolian people that I met seemed to have a particular fondness for people of Indian extraction and one of my close contacts, a woman called Soda Tensg, fluent in English and Russian, was so impressed with our humanitarian work that she promised to look for opportunities to become involved in the work of international aid agencies generally but in particular in India. I hoped that she would be successful.

The peripatetic life of flying around the world, staying three weeks at a time in each country, gave way to more traditional management consultancies – working on a bid to help develop Trinidad and Tobago health services and bidding for an allocation from the New Opportunities Fund to develop a Healthy Living Centre.

Working overseas gave me vast experience and versatility that would prove invaluable in future roles I would undertake.

Launch of Jhelum District Health Authority, Jhelum District, Punjab, Pakistan. Front row 3rd left author, 4th left Ismail Quershi, Punjab's Secretary Health, centre Nawabzada Syed Shams Haider, Member- Punjab's Provincial Assembly Chairman of Jhelum Health Authority.

Pakistani colleagues and British Council / Nuffield Institute for Health Leeds University staff - Second Family Health Project – on retreat Muree Hills – Punjab – Pakistan.

Pakistani Health Colleagues – Lahore – Pakistan – with Jacinthe Desmarais (second left standing).

Shalimar Gardens – Lahore – Pakistan, Mughal garden complex began in 1641 and completed a year later (obviously good project management!).

Meeting John Major – UK Prime Minister – British Council – Lahore.

Wagha border road crossing Pakistan/ India on the way to Amritsar and the Golden Temple (Harmandir Sahib) - 1995/96.

The Golden Temple (Harmandir Sahib) - 1995/96 - Amritsar - India.

Raj Ghat – memorial marking cremation spot of Gandhiji – new Delhi India.

Hawa Mahal – Wind Palace – Jaipur.

Inside Laxshmi Narayan Temple showing at the top the Svastika. A sacred and auspicious symbol used by many ancient civilisations, first appearing in Asia in the Indus Valley Civilisation C3000 BC. For Hindus it is one of the most important and widely used religious symbols.

The Nazis in Germany besmirched the history and peaceful manifestations of the symbol by twisting to the right its visual portrayal and using it on their flags badges and armbands for racist purposes.

The Taj Mahal – Agra. A pose made famous by Princess Diana on her visit to The Taj!

With Dr. Darakshan Badar and her husband having an English Afternoon Tea at Victory Services Club – London 2014.

Launch of District Management Teams for Multan, DG Khan and Bahawalpur Divisions- Directors, District Health Officers and their staff. Dr. Darakshan Badar (sitting second left) Author (standing third left).

CHAPTER 12

NATIONAL CONSULTANCIES

IN ROBBIE BURNS COUNTRY SCOTLAND

The next opportunity in July 1999 came, not from over the seas, but over the border in Scotland. I found this quite ironic as it's the home of the Argyll and Sutherland Highlanders and Black Watch soldiers, who had been sent to British Guiana in 1953 to arrest communists but had only found the red Hindu prayer flag flying, rather than the Communist one – the hammer and sickle! I thought I might come across survivors of that expedition or at least their families from associations with Guyanese women as wives or girlfriends.

Having been directly involved in closing the first and one of the largest learning disability hospital in the UK, Darenth Park, in Kent, I was the exact fit, as Project Director to lead a team to run down and close (termed retraction) the Royal Scottish National Hospital (RSNH) in Larbert, near Sterling. RSNH was opened in 1864 and was funded by 'pennies' from working class people and a £100 cheque from Queen Victoria. The original intention was for it to care and educate imbecile children between 6 and 12 years but, over the years, it gradually expanded to reach 1300 beds by 1967. During its development it was regarded as a Colony (self-sufficient in terms of food production and internal management). In the 1980s, with the change of emphasis from institutionalised to community care, patients were gradually moved out. By the time I got there the last tranche of 422 patients needed to be made ready for discharge.

Working on this £20 million Scottish Health Department centrally funded national project, had many advantages which the NHS could learn from. It was less hierarchical, consequently there was less bureaucracy and my impression was that there seemed to be more cohesiveness and national pride in identifying Scottish ways of doing things.

In common with many people from Guyana when I thought of going to live in England (in fact London) I never envisaged living or working in Scotland, Wales or Northern Ireland. My somewhat blinkered view was that the UK was mainly England. Many Guyanese genuinely believed that was where opportunities and prosperity lay. We knew of Scotland but considered it to be too cold and the people by and large dour and unwelcoming. Three years working in the country showed how very wrong this perception was. As I travelled the length and breadth of Scotland with my brand new leased Vauxhall Vectra, (running up 30,000 miles, eventually purchasing it a reasonable price and 16 years later still having it with me!). I found both professionally and socially a warm and friendly reception wherever I went. However, trying to persuade my social services colleagues that the financial packages we were transferring to them, to manage the ongoing care of the residents, was a huge challenge (secretly I had some sympathy with their predicament).

On the weather front, it was much colder than 'down south' but not nearly as cold as I had expected. Perhaps this was because I lived in a valley in Larbert/ Stirling area with the Ochil Hills in the distance. Snowfall lasted on the ground and roads much longer than in London (weeks rather days).

The task of gradually moving learning disability patients out of RSNH into communities brought up many of the issues which I had experienced 17 years earlier at Darenth Park. In particular securing appropriate accommodation was one of the biggest challenges due to 'the not in my backyard' prejudices of some local residents (reminding me of the early 1960s in London where some discriminated against people of colour). What was needed in specific cases were larger houses to accommodate several people who wanted to live together as these were scarce. One solution which proved to be effective was to negotiate with contractors of new housing schemes to provide a few larger units on their developments. Although we had to wait awhile for some properties to be finished, the solution was essentially successful as the discharged people were integrated into the community. As the patients were being moved out on a phased basis, the hospital's supporting services gradually slimmed down to reflect the reduced demand. As would be expected, this had a significant negative effect on staff, many of whom had worked at RSNH for several years. Redeployment elsewhere within Forth Valley Health Board and adjoining areas was therefore a priority, as was the support to those who chose to leave. It became clear that some patients were not physically well enough to be discharged into the community and for them we developed the initial plans for residual facilities. These were six ten- bedded bungalows for highly dependent patients which were subsequently built on part of the RSNH site and called Ochil Park. Also built on the site was the 850 bed Forth Valley Royal Hospital. Excellent example of adapting expensive NHS land to evolving healthcare clinical strategies.

By August 2002 the in-patient bed numbers had been considerably reduced and the main retraction programme, for me anyway, had come to a close. The Scottish Health Advisory Service on an end –of- project inspection commended the organisation and management as an 'exceptional achievement'. As Project Director these were warm words and reinforced my feelings of making a difference in healthcare despite not being a clinician.

Reflecting on the national recognition, which the Darenth Park closure had received I was disappointed that neither of the Chief Executives nor the Director of Social Services had, to my knowledge, received any awards such an OBE, Damehood etc. I wondered why there was this difference in national response to comparable achievements.

Many years later the work which had been done at RSNH, evidenced in the hospital records, and in the care of Stirling University, have been recognised by being added to the UNESCO UK Memory of the World register - promoting UK heritage across the world.

After successfully managing a major national programme I felt that re-entry at a top level in the NHS would be relatively easy. I was encouraged by being shortlisted for a number of Primary Care Trust Chief Executives' positions and a number of senior Directors' posts, all of which had the support of the two Chief Executives (CEs) in Scotland with whom I had been working. After a number of unsuccessful attempts, one of the CEs indirectly asked me what was the problem, hinting that perhaps I was being shortlisted to reflect equal opportunities considerations! One such short list for a Chief Executive's position in southern England caused me to ponder on this. I was the only person of colour on the shortlist and, at the Trust, could not see any Black or Asian people amongst the existing board members. The staff whom had been allocated to conduct pre- interview discussions and the assessor were also of a lighter hue. It became clear to me that, amongst a sea of pale faces in health and the wider community, I did not stand a chance for this particular position. The local candidate was appointed and I wondered whether the concern which had been expressed by one of my referees was correct. I decided never to travel another 517 miles for an experience of that nature!

"Peter Sahib, a very rewarding time in Scotland, did you see any of the Guyanese soldiers you mentioned or their relatives or perhaps the Loch Ness monster?"

"Alas, no, Basdeo the soldiers and Guyanese women seemed to have melted into Scottish society. Yes, I thought I saw the monster. Living in Larbert, I was very near to Loch Ness and on a misty morning it emerged and said that as both of you were mythical figures, it would be communicating with you directly."

"Peter Sahib, *I am lil bit vex wid your comparison and me na talking with you fo now, but please go ahead with your story*".

OK, Basdeo, I am sorry that you are upset with me and that you would not be talking with me for now. I will get you a vegetarian haggis and continue".

DEVELOPING PRIMARY CARE SERVICES

CYRIL SWEETT – HEALTHCARE CONSULTANCY

Whilst looking for a suitable placement in the NHS in England I was snapped-up by a private firm, called Cyril Sweett, who were developing their NHS interest in particular a joint venture development of community premises programme called Local Improvement Finance Trust (LIFT). Based in Gray's Inn Road, in London, Cyril Sweett engaged me to use my knowledge and experience to supplement their in- house team to secure NHS business across the board but mainly LIFT projects. No sooner had I settled into the partitioned open plan office (a significant change from my own office and secretary which I had grown accustomed to) than I had to accompany a colleague to King's Lynn, in East England, to present our bid for an interim Project Director's post to serve the three Primary Care Trusts in Norfolk. Presentation done, my colleague and I were driving out of the hospital, the mobile phone rang. A voice said:

"Can Peter start as soon as possible?"

"Yes, was the immediate reply" from my colleague.

There then followed a London to King's Lynn 106 miles (170 km) weekend commute and five week-day stays in a hotel. In four months of intensive work I was able to develop the urgent requirement, a Strategic Service Development Plan, gained signatures (and commitment) from the three Norfolk PCTs and the local Authority. I also identified £33million of first and second tranche capital building project schemes. The assignment was so successful that, although there was considerable doubt as to whether time scales would be met as it was the 'slack' period leading up to a Christmas /New Year break, the capital project notice (to start the contractual selection process) which needed to be placed in the Official Journal of the European Union (OJEU) by the end of the year was achieved. As some steps had to be taken which were not in accordance with instructions i.e. seeking approval before placing the notice, I had expected to receive the ire of the leader of the programme when Project Directors next met. However, my initiative gained commendation from Brian Johns, then Chief Executive of Partnership for Health, the Department of Health national coordinating body. Within a year having reached the age of 60 (the default extension to the retiring age a few years away) it was time to move on…again!

Wearing a kilt and holding a bagpipe – with Loch Ness monster behind me!
(Basdeo wanted to be in the picture but I refused!).

CHAPTER 13

BUILDING BETTER HEALTHCARE - FUTURE LEGACIES

SOUTHWEST LONDON AND ST. GEORGES –MENTAL HEALTH NHS TRUST - SPRINGFIELD HOSPITAL

St. George (of Lydda), the patron saint of England and a host of countries around the world and venerated by Catholics, Anglicans, eastern and oriental orthodox churches, has featured in many areas of my life. From my early childhood in Georgetown, to St. George's Anglican school to where I would now work at Southwest London and St. George's Mental Health NHS Trust (SWSTG). I was initially appointed as Project Director for the first of their major capital projects, using an innovative capital management process called Pro Cure 21, (short for Procurement in the twenty first century) How did I manage to get there?

In 42 continuous years in healthcare management and administration I had turned my hand to most things within my skills set and competencies. From ab inito medical orderly duties in the Royal Air Force I became adept at both operational and strategic management with an emphasis on tackling high profile projects. Having risen to the top of my profession in the NHS I deliberately chose to 'get off the ladder' and share my experience with colleagues and organisations in the developing world. I recognised that in so doing, getting back to the top level in the NHS would not be easy. This turned out to be accurate. But the satisfaction of making a difference to patient care where it was vitally needed (and in particular mentoring people who provided that care) compensated for any subsequent loss of status (and remuneration!). Having rationalised patient services and closed many hospitals in my time, I was now using my expertise to focus on managing the building of new healthcare facilities and hopefully leaving physical legacies for those who needed them.

St. George's was embarking on the first phase of a strategic plan to develop the 80 acre Springfield hospital site, to be called Springfield Village (integrating new healthcare facilities with new community residential and commercial uses). Situated in a prime location in an expensive area of Wandsworth Borough, the intention was to provide state-of- the art new mental health facilities for patients who were living in old buildings elsewhere on the site. Demolishing those buildings and in the process releasing excess land which could be used in the future to fund developments.

The headquarters of the Trust, Springfield University Hospital (its current name), had a long history. Following the Asylum Act of 1808 and the encouragement to build public asylums to avoid mentally ill people living on the streets, workhouses and private madhouses, the 97 acre Springfield Park was purchased in 1838 for £8,985 from a brewer to provide hospital accommodation. Tudor style buildings were constructed with ward wings at right angles coming off a central spinal corridor. It provided 350 beds at a cost of £67, 467. These were completed in 1840 and opened to patients in 1841 as the Surrey County Lunatic Asylum. Over the years, in common with many large mental health hospitals, the site was developed with additional buildings to reflect changes in models of care for mental health and learning disability patients. Surrounding land was turned into a farm with cows, poultry and pigs, with fruits from an orchard and a kitchen garden providing vegetables and salad. It was almost self-sufficient. In the First World War it became known as Springfield War Hospital and in the Second World War, patients were housed in the basements to avoid bombs. By the end of the war in 1945 the hospital had 2,040 patients and by 1948, when it joined the NHS that number had been reduced to 1,856.

THE PHOENIX UNIT
Approval to build the new unit was seen as a significant achievement in the Trust. According to local sources, the idea for a separate unit

was first discussed in 1987. It was strongly felt then that severely disabled long term clients required their own specialist rehabilitation unit. The suggestion that one of the wards vacated as a consequence of the development of community alternatives should be used on temporary basis was grasped and the Phoenix Unit was born. Subsequently, four attempts were made to provide a new unit, on each occasion overtaken by other more pressing needs. When new plans were developed there was much scepticism that this would be another false start. When 17 years later in 2004, the "Cutting of the Turf" (some calling it Turning the Sod!) event was held, to herald the beginning of work, there was general relief and joy within the Trust from patients, relatives and the wider community. The event itself was attended by local dignitaries including the Nigerian born councillor Chief Lola Ayorinde, who was the first black Mayor of the borough. She attended proudly dressed in what appeared to be a Nigerian national costume, including matching headwear and wearing the Wandsworth mayoral chain, designed in 1901 and often described as the finest in London. The Mayor was greeted on arrival by myself and a patient, I will call him Harry, who actually turned the turf with the Chairman of the Trust Jan Hildreth. The ceremony was attended by many people including the Regional General Manager of Integrated Health Project (IHP), the major construction contractor, Tom Barton, and the Director of Planning, Andrew Simpson.

My job - yet another high profile one - was to work with and lead a team of very dedicated and experienced individuals to provide, on time and within budget, the permanent Phoenix Unit (a title reflecting the building 'rising from the ashes'), a £7.2 million low secure high support two storey facility for 18 mental health rehabilitation patients. Prompt action was taken to appoint a Cost Adviser to support me as this would give the Trust Board the confidence that there was financial scrutiny in using the P21 process. Being a new system, there was some concern as to whether we would be getting value for money.

Using the Department of Health (DH) P21 framework meant that there was no need to seek bids through placing a notice in the Official Journal of European Union (OJEU), as was required by European regulations for all projects of this value. That work had already been done by the DH in setting up the framework. All that I needed to do was to invite Expressions of Interest from the twelve firms on the DH list, compile a shortlist, interview and then appoint a contractor. This process meant that within a short period of time (3 to 4 weeks) we would have a major contractor on board to start work - shaving at least three months off the normal tendering process with associated considerable reduction in paper work and bureaucracy. The P21 process offered a number of advantages – cost and time certainty, design and construction quality, financial security and skills development. The intention was to support the Trust to become 'Best Client' – staff acquiring the expertise and skills to manage major capital construction projects.

The successful Principal Supply Chain Partner (PSCP), a term used to describe the main building contractor was IHP, a joint venture between Sir Robert McAlpine and Norwest Holst who brought with them Nightingale Architects in the person of an Architect called Karen Flatt.

The success of any project depends on fostering efficient and effective working relationships between the client and the provider. Friendship was a bonus. I was fortunate in developing this with IHP Project Manager, John Fraser. He and I felt that we had something to prove. Not only was this the first P21 project in the London area, it was also the first for IHP and was therefore seen as a flagship project for the Trust, IHP and P21 nationally. Our every action would be scrutinised and success would bring credit to both parties and, for IHP, the possibility of further work. John, a much younger man, impressed me with the depth of his technical knowledge and his ability to keep calm under pressure.

A testing time came when, through one of those unfortunate incidents that happen from time to time when carrying out construction work on an active hospital sites, power or water supplies are interrupted. Our incident involved the incorrect connection of a standby generator, damaging the power supply to large parts of the hospital. Not being an acute patient care areas with crucial electrically powered equipment, meant that the direct effect on clinical care was not as severe as it could have been. Nevertheless it could have had a negative effect on the reputation of the contactor and the new P21 process (there was and remained for a time some scepticism about the framework).Areas directly affected included the administrative block and the finance department, the latter falling into the category of needing to be convinced of the efficacy of P21! John quickly accepted liability, set in train the process for expeditious insurance compensation to replace the damaged equipment and reputations were salvaged!

John and I and our respective teams, NHS and P21 contactors, felt that this first building, with its proximity to listed buildings on the site and with our emphasis on providing homely accommodation, should make a statement which others would follow. Avant garde processes in all aspects of project delivery were considered to be important and we felt that the building's circular curved design construction plan would enhance patient observation and staff safety. The structure was also designed to maximise daylight and views of the gardens and landscaping. Zinc was used for the roofing to simulate lead, over a period of time, with red brick outer walls and red cedar panels. A hard landscaped courtyard with a large raised planted bed of flowers enabled residents, sitting on the benches provided, to experience a wide range of scents coming from lavender, honeysuckle and other plants and, when the weather was good, even to have a barbeque.

During construction and mindful of keeping the project on time and within budget, the provision of bathroom pods (pre-assembled compact units providing shower, wash hand basin and toilet) was felt to be needed urgently. After researching local UK suppliers we were advised that units were available in Venice, Italy, subject to personal inspection and agreement as to suitability. Visions of business class flights and an overnight stay in this World Heritage city were soon dashed. What happened in reality was that we travelled there and back in one day on a budget airline flight. On arrival we were taken by taxi along a motorway toward Venice where the company was based in the 'aircraft hangar' building housing the pods, inspection and assessment and back to London! The Grand Canal, gondolas and St. Mark's Square would have to wait for another occasion. We approved the pods assisted by personal testing by Gary Tubman, our nursing representative on the team. All 18 pods were delivered on time, despite the 965miles (1553km) journey, dropped in by a crane into the prepared spaces and were quickly connected to the other services in the building – a good example of co-operation in handling a potential crisis!

To manage the project and to keep stakeholders involved I formed a Project Board comprising the key stakeholders including, very importantly, medical and nursing staff and representatives of the users and carers. Gary, the nursing representative, a Yorkshire man, played a crucial role in ensuring that the design of the building reflected the care needs of the residents and the aspirations of the clinical staff. He physically tested installations. On one occasion when he was unable to operate the sample door handles that were being provided (Gary was a rugby playing man!) the sample was rejected and a model more suitable for use by less robust nursing and residents hands, were supplied. The user carer representative, I will call him Harold , played an equally important role as he opened and sustained a communication channel between the project team and the users which resulted in a number of design improvements, including the provision of art work and an artificial frog for the water feature in the courtyard. Harold penned a beautiful, and humorous end-of-project poem in recognition of his involvement in, and contribution to project challenges. Comparing the project to a ship at sea sailing through potentially stormy waters, he gave nautical names to key players - including me as Admiral Ram and Gary Tubman as Captain Tub. The poem highlighted that, despite the storm and tempest, we had come through together as friends. It ended with a mixed metaphor suggesting that a mythical bird (Phoenix) had become a successful boat!

Praise also came from the Patients' Forum which, following a visit, said that "we were very impressed with the design of the building, the spacious airy well lit banana (sic) shaped corridor, the roomy bedrooms which all looked out onto the gardens and the large dining room and activity rooms which opened onto a lovely interior courtyard garden." We were all thrilled by this excellent endorsement which confirmed to us that genuine patients and carer involvement in the provision of the accommodation and services paid handsome dividends.

Within a year of turning the turf, the project was completed and four days after my 62nd birthday it was jointly opened on 14th October 2005, by the local MP for Tooting, Sadiq Khan, and a male resident, I will call him Joseph. He was chosen to represent other users and in recognition of the importance of the users involvement in the development of the facility.

Sadiq, from a Muslim background, was elected MP in the same year and would go on to become a leading member of the Labour party in government as Minister of State for Communities (2008/9), Minister of State for Transport (2009/10) and when Labour went into opposition Shadow Secretary of State for Transport (2010) and Shadow Secretary of State for Justice/ Shadow Lord Chancellor and currently (2015) being touted as a future candidate for Mayor of London to replace the Conservative's Boris Johnson.

Also present at the opening ceremony was the then Mayor of Wandsworth, Councillor Diana Whitingham (who by now had replaced Councillor Ayorinde through the annual Mayoral election process) and a wide range of representatives from patient groups, the community, Trust Board, Strategic Health Authority, neighbouring Primary Care Trusts, contractors and other Trust staff including Dee McEvoy, a long serving member of the Planning Department. She was one of those special persons in every Trust with a fountain of institutional knowledge who could be relied upon to effectively troubleshoot whenever necessary. Dee gave me a very warm welcome when I first joined the Trust (we had initially shared an office whilst mine was made ready), had been a tremendous support and confidant throughout my time there and was a key contributing member to the project. On its success Dee said "To me it was a bit like baking a cake really, everyone had their own ingredient to add, all into one big bowl, some mixing to take place, not forgetting a little stir and the result a wonderful rich cake, with amazing icing to top it off." The sentiments expressed in this comment were confirmed when the Project was recognised as a finalist in the Team of the Year Award in the Trust Quality Awards for 2005 and being commended in the Wandsworth Borough Council Design Award 2005. Andrew Simpson, The Director of Planning, Karen Flatt, Architect and I were pleased to attend a ceremony at the Council to receive the Award.

Having joined the Trust in November 2003 as an Interim Project Director, I was appointed following NHS recruitment procedures to the permanent post. I led the development of the Business Case (the process through which the capital or cost of a major project and the running or revenue expenditure of that scheme are examined thoroughly and explained) through the various levels of approval. I had also delivered the first fully in-house managed major capital project, in 19 months, on time and within the £7.2million budget using the new P21 process. I felt that the Trust Board was satisfied with the outcome. More importantly the residents (patients), their relatives and staff were pleased with what had been achieved.

In a pre-completion review by the Future Healthcare Network, based on the Royal College of Psychiatrists' publication 'Not Just Bricks and Mortar', we were pleased to highlight what had been done to address the therapeutic environment and security and safety for residents. The provision of a choice of communal rooms, the progressive manner in which accommodation was provided allowing residents to move from single en-suite bedrooms to one of the three en-suite bedsits with kitchenette, as they were being prepared for discharge into the community.

The 'Venetian' pods were given special attention not only for their in-built anti ligature features (structurally designed to avoid areas where patients could harm themselves) but also their contribution to the time the scale of the building programme.

CANADIAN INVITATION - P21 PRESENTATION

International recognition of our work came in 2007 when I was invited by a Professor of Project Management and Sustainable Construction, Daniel Forgues of CERACQ (The Centre for Studies and Research for the Advancement of the Construction Industry in Quebec), to make a presentation at a conference in Montreal, Canada. Daniel was in the UK pursuing a PhD and the Department of Health had recommended the Phoenix Project as one which would provide valuable research material.

John Fraser had moved on from IHP to Mace, another major construction firm, but permission was obtained from both organisations for John to join me (this in itself was an indication of the cooperation which had been engendered with contractors using P21 framework). The title of our joint presentation 'Challenging Convention' (which CERACQ uploaded on Google and it is still there!) was very well received and our Canadian colleagues were intrigued to hear how effective partnership worked, whilst maintaining the healthy tension between client and provider to keep project costs under control. We left the conference believing that the delegates were seriously considering how the process might be adapted for use in Quebec in general and Montreal in particular. A good example of sharing best practice, a key feature of the P21 process I would say.

FURTHER ESTATE DEVELOPMENTS
Nothing stands still in life and perhaps the NHS in the UK is one of the best examples of this. Changes of government very often result in new initiatives being introduced in government departments and the NHS, as part of the Department of Health, seemed to have a disproportionate amount of organisational upheavals. One consequence of these changes was a constant turnover of NHS senior staff, with the average time in post of current chief executives reported to be around three years.

At St. George's, between the start of the Phoenix Unit and its completion, both the Chief Executive and the Chairman had left. It was therefore necessary to get new leaders to commit to previously agreed strategies. The Estate Strategy (proposals to provide safe, secure, high quality healthcare buildings) was a particular challenge as it needed to be developed to follow the service strategy (plans for organising and delivering clinical services). Flexibility to accommodate new models of care, emerging technologies and perennial financial constraints were key considerations.

Having a senior person involved in a major project who remained in-post while some of the top leaders moved on, could be beneficial for a number of reasons. He/she could provide authoritative background information on strategies and decisions which had been taken but which might not be fully evident from reading papers. People in the NHS described this as institutional memory (the loss of which was attributed to constant changes). It was felt that the senior person could, in particular, communicate the vision which had been previously developed to new leaders and hopefully gain their commitment.

I found these qualities in a colleague, Andrew Simpson, the Director of Planning, a Cambridge University graduate who had known of, and had worked in, the Trust for several years and had a deep understanding and appreciation of the needs of service users and the views of service providers. Andrew had a clear vision of what was required to develop the entire 80 acre site and a missionary zeal in challenging the existing norms in the provision of mental health accommodation. His determination, resilience and leadership persuaded the Trust Board and in particular the Chairman Jan Hildreth, and Chief Executive Dr. Nigel Fisher, to support the initial phase of this dynamic programme. Andrew played a pivotal role in gaining continued commitment from the Trust Board in general, and the new leaders in particular, John Rafferty, Chairman and Peter Houghton, Chief Executive.

By 2006 the delivery of the Phoenix Unit had been accomplished. The successful completion of a Strategic Outline Case (the first stage of the Business Case process) for the redevelopment of the Springfield Hospital site and approval of the Full Business Case secured. The next major capital project, the Wandsworth Acute Unit (since changed to Wandsworth Recovery Centre) meant, among other things, the formal establishment of Springfield Regeneration Programme Board. I became Director of Major Capital Projects with responsibility 'to prepare and implement (as an accredited Projects Director) the building capital programme associated with the redevelopment ….and senior managerial responsibility for operational aspects of estates and facilities'. This essentially widened my initial remit.

WANDSWORTH RECOVERY CENTRE

With a number of 1840 buildings on the site, some listed (in the UK a building or structure which is considered to be of 'special architectural or historical interest') Wandsworth Recovery Centre replaced the 1931 Bluebell ward, used for acute psychiatric admissions and the 1886 John Meyer ward used for psychiatric intensive care. The project cost £23 million and provided 10 intensive care beds, an 18 bed mixed gender in –patient facility for adults with acute mental illness, outpatient facilities and office space for mental health outreach teams.

The confidence gained from the successful use of the P21 framework meant that, as the rules existed at that time, the Trust could invite the Phoenix contractor, Integrated Health Projects, to work on this second project without the need to go out to further competitive tendering- a considerable selection advantage. All of the challenges in the first project existed on this second but there were additional pressures.

The John Meyer ward was a 120 years old anachronism. Whilst clinical care moved with the times, the physical structure did not lend itself to easy adaptation to suit current requirements. Coupled with this there was unfavourable publicity arising from serious incidents; a fatality on, and escapes from, the ward which led to, among other things, for its urgent replacement to be a priority for the Trust to meet the requirements of, amongst others, the Mental Health Act Commission (in time to be incorporated into the Care Quality Commission) the regulatory body.

Confident that by using the P21 framework I would be able to deliver what was needed on time and within budget, I set about forming an effective multi discipline project team. Cost advice and project management were provided by Mike Penny and Robin Bruce from MF projects. Mike had worked with me on the Phoenix project and I had high regard for his professional knowledge and his ability to challenge when needed. Robin provided timely and meticulous analysis of trends, in particular those that were going the wrong way. He also had an engaging manner when resolving issues.

To ensure that all our construction and design management (CDM) issues were addressed, I engaged Norman King of King Safety Services who had considerable experience and could be relied on to ensure that we fully complied with CDM regulations. To a greater extent than Phoenix, in part because we were providing a psychiatric intensive care unit, it was imperative to have a clinically trained person as a permanent member of my direct team and she came in the form of a woman called Susan Muir. She was a very experienced senior nurse who had worked elsewhere in the Trust with good connections with colleagues. Susan, became my right hand person on clinical issues playing a significant role in developing models of care, operational policies and gaining acceptance from the medical and nursing staff. To complete my direct reports was my personal assistant Beverly Wills. Bev had been at the Trust for many years, had tremendous institutional knowledge and the ability to re-route unwanted callers with grace, either on the telephone or in person, especially when we were involved in crisis meetings. Members of this core group of six led or were involved in eight specific task sub groups - clinical reference, interior design, user/carer, communications, design, risk, finance and project progress.

Although not directly responsible to me, three consultant psychiatrists, who were tremendously supportive to me personally and to the projects in general, were Dr. Rosemary Ball and Dr. Charlotte Harrison for Phoenix and Dr. Frances Raphael for Wandsworth Recovery Centre. Despite their significant clinical workload they found the time to attend numerous project group meetings. They also helped to develop new models of care and operational policies and generally linked the consultants' group to the activities of the project. Frances often went the extra mile by regularly sitting through what were probably boring meetings listening to detailed building material-type issues. But her interest and commitment never waned and we could rely on her to steer us through clinical operational topics. We were all most grateful for the significant contribution she made to the project's success.

To succeed with any clinically focused project in the NHS it is imperative to gain consultants' commitment, as 'product champions'. This was something we certainly had.

"Peter Sahib, why have you given such technical and what some might consider detailed information about the structure of the project and the personnel involved?"

"Well Basdeo, it is good to recognise those who have made significant contribution to my success at certain parts of my life and these people certainly did. Furthermore, others might be interested in knowing how this major capital project was set up and the team spirit which was engendered"

"OK, thanks Peter Sahib, please continue."

The main Wandsworth Recovery Centre construction started in August 2007 and was completed and handed over to the Trust in April 2009 but not without a little drama. Nearing the end of the project we were suddenly advised by the regulatory body that we needed to raise the surrounding wall height of the building from 4.8 to 5.2metres to enable the unit to accommodate a number of patients who might require this degree of protection. Mindful that significant delay would fall foul of the commitment which had been given to the Mental Health Act Commission and that the cost would exceed the Trust's part of Guaranteed Maximum Price (GMP –a significant feature of the P21 framework), effective collaboration another crucial aspect of the framework, came into play. The GMP was upwardly revised, allowed by the framework, as the Trust had changed the specification, and the additional work was carried out with minor slippage. This meant that Regulatory Body's deadline was met. Everyone breathed a sigh of relief.

The state of the art project included all the features of a modern mental health unit - large open spaces, flexible activity areas, sports pitch and gym and a range of therapeutic and safe facilities. IHP, the main contractor, engaged a wide range of P21 framework members, including MAAP Architects and, in particular, Mungo Smith who had gained a national reputation for designing mental health facilities.

Our joint efforts were recognised when we won the national Building Better Health Care Award 2009 for Best Project Team and commended for Mental Healthcare Design. Most of team were delighted to attend the Award Ceremony at a posh function in the City of London. In 2010 we also won the International Design and Health Academy Award for Health Unit, seeing off competition from across the globe. The award recognised international excellence in the field of design and health. All of us engaged on the project were extremely pleased.

"Peter Sahib, you have recounted many of the enjoyable experiences in your work at St. George's but you have not mentioned any of the work difficulties you experienced.

"Yes Basdeo, but I have deliberately chosen not to go into those because with the passage of time they have faded into the distance when compared to really positive achievements. Secondly, I am satisfied that the visible testimony of what I did at St. George's was to the lead the development of two state of the art buildings – Phoenix Unit and Wandsworth Recovery Centre. I managed in a tightly controlled, effective and efficient manner £30 million of public money which would improve the care of mentally ill people and the buildings should last for at least another 40 to 50 years. In so doing my projects colleagues and I had laid the foundation for the further development of the Springfield Hospital site into the proposed Springfield Village. That's tremendous satisfaction and overcome any other residual negative experiences or emotions"

"Thanks Peter Sahib, please continue"

Phoenix Unit – Project Team members, L. to R. Joe Phillips, John Fraser, author, Neil Harnett and colleague.

Phoenix Unit – receiving Wandsworth Borough Council Design Award 2005 L to R Andrew Simpson, Councillor Ravi Govindia, Karen Flatt and colleague from Nightingale Architects and author.

Canadian hosts – Challenging Convention – John Fraser (second left) author (centre) Professor Daniel Forgues (far right).

Wandsworth Recovery Centre Project Team L. to R. Norman King, Robin Bruce, Mike Penny, Susan Muir and Bev Wills (sitting).

Stuart Thomson, Borough Director receiving keys to Wandsworth Recovery Centre from Richard Noel IHP Project Manager (who had replaced John Fraser on this project).

Wandsworth Recovery Centre Project Team members receiving the Building Better Healthcare Building Award – London.

Headquarters of Southwest London and St. George's Mental Health NHS Trust - Springfield University Hospital - where I worked 2003 - 2009.

Wandsworth Recovery Centre.

Phoenix Unit.

Plaque recording the opening of the the Phoenix Unit
and the personnel involved.

CHAPTER 14

AWARDS/ROYAL INVITATIONS

NHS LONG SERVICE AWARD

In addition to awards achieved for the two projects which I had led, I also received three personal awards.

The first was at the Trust's annual recognition of staff who had achieved outstanding performances which also included those who had worked for over 20 years in the NHS. Although I had completed the required period in 1990 whilst at Dartford and Gravesham, that Health Authority did not have such arrangements. I was therefore very pleased to be included, albeit 14 years after the event, in the list of exceptional achievers and had pleasure in receiving my certificate and gift of a crystal decanter and glasses from the Chairman of the Trust, John Rafferty. These award ceremonies, now being held around the NHS are an indication of the value being placed on health service staff and serve as morale boosting incentives.

INSTITUTE OF HEALTHCARE MANAGEMENT - COMPANIONSHIP

The second award was from the Institute of Healthcare Management (IHM) – 'the leading independent membership organisation for health and care managers across the UK, supporting personal development and driving change to improve health and wellbeing for all.' IHM traced its history to 1902 when a number of hospital officers founded the Hospital Officers' Association. The original aim was to create a supportive social and professional forum where colleagues could meet from time to time to share ideas and network. Over the years the Association's role, structure, membership and name changed, the latter to reflect the move from health *service administration* to *healthcare management* in the UK health services.

IHM also introduced educational programmes - the Diploma in Hospital Administration changed to the Diploma in Health Services Management and Certificates in Management Studies and Managing Health Services, the latter two in conjunction with the Open University.

Royal patronage was obtained in the person of Her Royal Highness, the Princess Royal in 1960 then latterly in 1972 by His Royal Highness Prince Phillip, Duke of Edinburgh, the husband of the Queen.

Membership of the IHM was considered to be an essential requirement for anyone seeking a senior administrative/management position in the NHS. Membership grades were Licentiate, Associate, Fellow and Companionship, reflecting qualifications and experience.

I joined the IHM in 1977 as someone passionately concerned with continuous professional development and succession planning. I served on the South East England, Scotland and London Regional Councils of the Institute for several years. During that time I played a very active part in promoting the work of the Institute and general management training. It was therefore an honour to gain the highest recognition of the Institute - the award of Companionship for my 'significant contribution to healthcare management and the Institute'. At a posh ceremony held in 2003 at the Manchester United Football Ground International Suite, I was very proud to receive my certificate from the President of the Institute, Dr. Gerry McSorley.

Companionship is only awarded to 2% of the membership of the Institute. I would now join a select group of Companions which included Sir David Nicholson, the former, Chief Executive of the National Health Service in England, Dame Ruth Carnall, the former Chief Executive of NHS London and a coterie of high achievers in my sector. It is a special sense of satisfaction (and humility) when your colleagues in your own profession recognise you in this way.

My involvement with the Institute has continued and I was appointed Chair of the London (now including Southern England) Regional Council in 2007 and remained in this position as it continued its development. As the NHS was going through considerable change in 2013/14 one of our priorities was to create an environment where the leaders in the Department of Health (DH) and the National Health Service could share with IHM members the key issues of the day followed by lively questions and answers. A number of informal evening sessions were organised, attended by several members of the top team at the DH including Dame Barbara Hakin, Managing Director of Commissioning Development, Ian Dalton, CBE, Chief Operating Officer of the NHS Commissioning Board and its Deputy Chief Executive and Mike Farrar, CBE, Chief Executive of the NHS Confederation, the membership body for organisations that make up the NHS. We have continued with this trend and following the implementation of the Health and Social Care Act 2012 we were pleased when Duncan Selby, the new Chief Executive of Public Health England, attended one of our sessions to share his views of public health in the restructured DH/NHS and celebrate the public launch of our joining with the Royal Society for Public Health in 2012. Adding to the support our members had received from this array of senior leaders was Simon Stevens, Chief Executive of NHS England. Simon had been appointed to this position in April 2014, and it was a great delight for us to welcome him ten months into the new job particularly after he and other healthcare leaders had published one of the most important health and social care policy documents in England in recent years – The NHS Five Years Forward View. This document sets out a vision for the future of the NHS and articulates why change is needed, what that change might like look like and how it can be achieved. The document received overwhelming support within the sector and went some way to repair the perceived damage caused by the Health and Social Care Act 2012.

ROYAL INVITATIONS

Public appreciation of contributions to your fellow citizens come in different forms. A personal 'thank you' to someone you had particularly helped or recognition by your professional peers is gratifying especially when you have not set out to achieve this. In the

UK, a constitutional monarchy, there are time honoured processes for recognising achievers through the Queen's annual birthday and New Year's honours. Another acknowledgement is to be invited to an event hosted by the Queen or other members of the Royal Family.

Mine came in the 1985 when I was invited to Kensington Palace to meet Prince Charles and Princess Diana. As I understood it the reason for the invitation (at the time I was a senior health service manager and a Justice of the Peace) was for the newly married couple to meet with a wide range of ordinary people in the community, especially those from an ethnic minority background (the presence at the reception of relatively large representation from this group an indication that this might have been the purpose) However, I never found out authoritatively why I was invited and felt no burning desire to do so. I was just glad to receive the invitation.

The reception was most enjoyable with lots to eat and drink and an opportunity to network. As would be expected everyone in the room edged their way towards the host to have a few words. This was an interesting foot shuffling exercise as surreptitious action was called for so as not to appear overtly 'pushy'. You were reminded by a gentle prod on your elbow by one of the 'assistants' if you appeared to be taking more than one or two minutes with the Royals. It was clearly designed for the Royal couple to move around the room and talk to as many people as possible.

My next invitation came on 21st July 2011. This was to the Queen's Garden Party. I was much clearer about why I was invited to this event as I knew it was a simple way of rewarding and recognising those who had shown dedication to public services and charity work.

Armed with the unusually large cardboard-stiff invitation I headed for Buckingham Palace to join thousands of people (all dressed in their finest clothes) who were eager to have a chance of meeting (or at least seeing!) not only the Queen, but also other senior members of the Royal family who joined Her Majesty on these occasions. The grounds of the Palace were exactly what I expected. They were exquisitely manicured with ample space to accommodate thousands of invitees. We were lined up in rows, with sufficient gap to allow the Royal Party to circulate. They would stop from time to time to have a chat. It was clear that everyone including me was trying to catch one of the Royals' attention in the hope of engaging in a fleeting but memorable conversation. Failing that, at least having the satisfaction of seeing the Royal Party close up. There was an adequate supply of tea, coffee and sandwiches, laid out on long tables in buffet form. The sandwiches were daintily cut into small triangles, with a variety of luxurious fillings including smoked salmon and prawns. The hot drinks were served in china tea cups.

July in England is often sunny and warm. On this occasion the weather was disappointing. Very shortly after the event started the heavens opened up. There was thunder and lightning. Guests dodged from tree to tree trying to avoid being struck, most were aiming to get into the already crowded marquees placed around the garden. I felt that the monsoons had followed me from Pakistan and I was not best pleased. The storm eventually subsided and we returned to the refreshments and networking. Altogether, quite an experience!

"Peter Sahib, good examples of your awards, voluntary work and rubbing shoulders with the good and the great"

"Yes Basdeo, how very observant, I will return to my story!"

Receiving NHS Long Service award from John Rafferty -Chairman of South West London and St. George's Mental Health NHS Trust.

Receiving Institute of Healthcare Management Companionship Award from Gerry Mc Sorley, President of the Institute.

Launch of joint Institute of Healthcare Management /Royal Society of Public Health working with L to R Professor Richard Parish, Chief Executive – RSPH, author, Duncan Selbie, Chief Executive, Public Health England and Dr. Patricia Riordan, Director of Public Health.

IHM Speed Networking with left Rachael Patterson, Director of People and Organisational Development, North Middlesex Hospital, Bob Heald, Partner, Gardiner & Theobald, Jan Filochowski, Chief Executive Great Ormond Street Hospital, author, Ian Wilson, Chief Executive, Southwest London & St. George's Mental Health Trust and Mike Farrar, Chief Executive, NHS Confederation. April 2002.

Members of IHM London and South of England Regional Council with Simon Stevens, Chief Executive, NHS England – L to R Gordon Pownall, James Chal, Simon Stevens, author, Jill De Bene. February 2015.

On the way to Buckingham Palace Garden Party. July 2011 (a bright start - thunder and lighting came after!).

CHAPTER 15

VOLUNTARY SERVICE OVERSEAS

IN THE LONG SHADOWS OF KILIMANJARO

MASASI, TANZANIA

During six years at South West London and St. George's Mental Health NHS Trust I continued with my voluntary work.

Working as a consultant in developing countries increased my awareness of the challenges faced by governments as they battle to provide good standards of education, work opportunities and health for their people with diminishing resources. I decided to dedicate part of my holidays to provide my knowledge, skills and experience wherever it was needed but in particular in Africa. I registered my interest with British Executive Service Overseas (BESO) - which has since been merged with Voluntary Service Overseas (VSO). BESO's aim was to promote volunteering to fight global poverty and disadvantage. By sharing skills, creativity and learning they sought to build a fairer world. Their six development goals were: education, HIV and AIDS, disability, health, secure livelihoods and participation. BESO concentrated on sending the more experienced volunteers to help developing countries. Their mission statement and objectives struck a chord with me and I was pleased to be selected to go to Tanzania to help the Bishop and Diocese of Masasi, in the south east region of the country.

The Diocese had strong connections with Britain as the late Archbishop Trevor Huddleston, a fierce and well known anti-apartheid campaigner, was consecrated Bishop of Masasi in 1968. Continuing UK interest came in the form of support provided by the Diocese of Hereford and the Friends of Masasi living in different parts of the UK.

The area covered by the Diocese is one of the poorest parts of the country and it is estimated that about 36% of the population falls below the national poverty line and 43% are unable to maintain a minimum daily intake of dietary energy. Intermittent drought exacerbates an already fragile local economy. As part of their Christian mission, the Diocese was involved in empowering communities to be self-sufficient including providing support to farmers. One of the initiatives was to enhance the health services provided by the state by supporting the development of dispensaries, which in addition to providing primary care services also had some in-patient bed facilities for emergencies. The Diocese also supported Mkomaindo Hospital in Masasi town which had a special place in the heart of its parishioners as they played a crucial role its development. The hospital was once in the private sector then transferred to Government control. The possibility of it being returned to the private sector was being explored.

My first trip to Tanzania in the autumn of 2001 was as an Organisational Analysis Specialist to assess the capability of the Diocese to take a greater part in the management of Mkomaindo Hospital. I received a very warm welcome from Bishop Patrick Mwachiko, his wife Emmy and the Diocesan officers. I was treated as an honoured guest rather than a professional coming to look at their management style and capacity. I was given every assistance in conducting the 17 day study. The workshop arranged to gather information reminded me of the experience I'd had in another African country, Botswana, where led by a chief or headman, community decisions are arrived at by consensus. In this case the Bishop played that important role.

It became apparent that with their other responsibilities, lack of human resources and hospital management skills, the Diocese could not immediately take a greater part in the management of the hospital. In making a number of institutional strengthening recommendations I suggested that the Diocese concentrated on providing assistance to one particular area of the hospital Maternity Services, as this would reflect priority concerns in the district.

In the summer of 2003 I returned to Masasi for two weeks , this time as a Volunteer Programme Leader with the remit to help local communities work together to improve their livelihoods. Called the 'Masasi Together Programme' it also involved linking the Diocese to voluntary consultancy work which BESO was carrying out on Agriculture and HIV/AIDs. Professional expertise in organisational analysis and institutional strengthening were the skills required. The successful assignment was followed up two years later, in the summer of 2005, to continue and update previous recommendations and to prepare a draft constitution for a Trust. This was being formed to bring together the recommendations from the three consultancy areas. I also focused on developing operational guidelines, roles and responsibilities and fund raising.

The recommendations were well received and assistance in their implementation was given from the UK through internet exchanges.

"Peter Sahib, where are you now with this voluntary work?"

"Basdeo, I continued with my voluntary support to Masasi Diocese, now split into two with Newala, another area in the region having its own Bishop. I gained enormous satisfaction from being able to share, in a voluntary capacity, the skills and experience I had acquired. I have benefited enormously from the experience. From the feedback and contacts that have been maintained, I feel the recipients were also satisfied with the outcomes."

"Thanks, Peter Sahib"

HELPING HANDS ACROSS THE SEAS

GUYHEALTH (UK)

Assistance to Guyana's Health Service also continued and on a visit to the UK by their then Minister of Health, Dr. Leslie Ramsammy, I organised for him and His Excellency Laleshwar Singh, Guyana's High Commissioner to the UK, to meet with the Trust's Chairman, Jan Hildreth and Dr. Nigel Fisher, Chief Executive. This opened the opportunity for supportive twinning arrangements, between St. George's Mental Health Trust and Guyana's health services. We also met with Peter Homa, Chief Executive at St. George's Care

Trust (Acute Services), with the intention of pursuing the same aim. Twenty years later the formal aims are still to be fully realised but the seeds were sown in the organisational minds of both parties. We also met with senior people at the London School of Hygiene and Tropical Medicine, the world's leading research-focused graduate school. The purpose was to explore setting up distance learning programmes for Guyanese students. It was felt that this would be more economic than sending graduates to the UK and would also allow study in a home environment. Much interest and potential for development were expressed. As with the twinning prospects, Guyhealth (UK) facilitated the links and left the Ministry of Health to continue the development, becoming directly involved as and when further support was needed.

'Atlantic Dash Gives Old Beds New Life' - that was the headline in the local newspaper Wandsworth Borough News reporting on further assistance to Guyana which is always in need of hospital supplies to supplement their own resources. The Guyanese diaspora in the UK and elsewhere are always on the lookout for useable items which could be put to good use in the country. As a number of hospital beds and other supplies were becoming redundant at Springfield Hospital, (part of South West London and St. George's Mental Health NHS Trust), I obtained permission for the items to be gifted to Guyana's Health Service. There then followed the type of voluntary collaboration and support (to the developing world) for which Britain is especially known around the globe. The 17 beds and mattresses were collected from Springfield Hospital by SOLK, a furniture company who had dealings with the Trust, and transported on two separate occasions to the port of Felixstowe nearly 100 miles away. The first stage was achieved without cost to us.

As our charity did not have the resources needed for taking the consignment to Guyana, we sought a shipping agent who would provide this service for free. After extensive searching we found one, but just when we were about to put the arrangements into place they pulled out. Frantic, as storage costs for the consignment were mounting at Felixstowe, Europe West Indies Lines stepped in and the cargo was sent the 4,500miles to Guyana. We were all pleased that the entire process, including the personnel involved, was provided as a donation.

Invited to comment by the press I said that: "it is gratifying that these beds will now be put to good use in a developing country that is doing its utmost to provide the best possible healthcare under extreme financial pressure. The fact that people and companies in this country wanted to be part of the process is not only heartening but shows that where people's health, welfare and future are concerned, co-operation knows no boundaries." Small though it was, this was another example of the many ways in which Britain continues to support the developing world.

With Bishop Patrick Mwachiko, Bishop of Masasi and his wife Emmy on visit to the UK – Greenwich Park London.

With Project counterparts discussing health, HIV/AIDs /Agricutural issues – Masasi Tanzania. 2001-2003-2005.

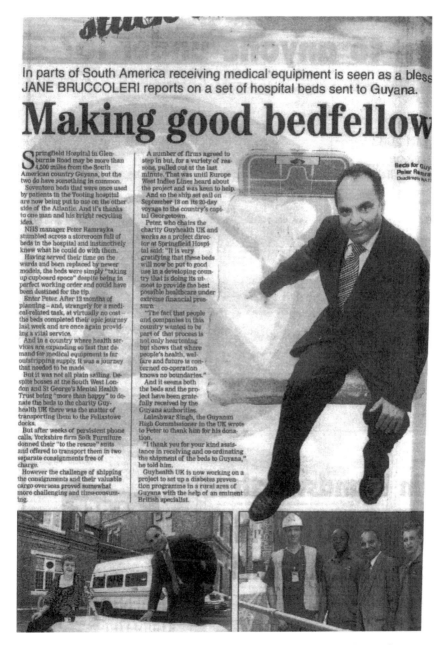

In parts of South America receiving medical equipment is seen as a bless
JANE BRUCCOLERI reports on a set of hospital beds sent to Guyana.

Making good bedfellow

Springfield Hospital in Glenburnie Road may be more than 4,500 miles from the South American country Guyana, but the two do have something in common.

Seventeen beds that were once used by patients in the Tooting hospital are now being put to use on the other side of the Atlantic. And it's thanks to one man and his bright recycling idea.

NHS manager Peter Ramrayka stumbled across a storeroom full of beds in the hospital and instinctively knew what he could do with them.

Having served their time on the wards and been replaced by newer models, the beds were simply "taking up cupboard space" despite being in perfect working order and could have been destined for the tip.

Enter Peter. After 12 months of planning – and, strangely for a medical-related task, at virtually no cost – the beds completed their epic journey last week and are once again providing a vital service.

And in a country where health services are expanding so fast that demand for medical equipment is far outstripping supply, it was a journey that needed to be made.

But it was not all plain sailing. Despite bosses at the South West London and St George's Mental Health Trust being "more than happy" to donate the beds to the charity Guyhealth UK there was the matter of transporting them to the Felixstowe docks.

But after weeks of persistent phone calls, Yorkshire firm Solk Furniture donned their "to the rescue" suits and offered to transport them in two separate consignments free of charge.

However the challenge of shipping the consignments and their valuable cargo overseas proved somewhat more challenging and time-consuming.

A number of firms agreed to step in but, for a variety of reasons, pulled out at the last minute. That was until Europe West Indies Lines heard about the project and was keen to help.

And so the ship set sail on September 18 on its 20-day voyage to the country's capital Georgetown.

Peter, who chairs the charity Guyhealth UK and works as a project director at Springfield Hospital said: "It is very gratifying that these beds will now be put to good use in a developing country that is doing its utmost to provide the best possible healthcare under extreme financial pressure.

"The fact that people and companies in this country wanted to be part of that process is not only heartening but shows that where people's health, welfare and future is concerned co-operation knows no boundaries."

And it seems both the beds and the project have been gratefully received by the Guyana authorities.

Laleshwar Singh, the Guyanan High Commissioner in the UK wrote to Peter to thank him for his donation.

"I thank you for your kind assistance in receiving and co-ordinating the shipment of the beds to Guyana," he told him.

Guyhealth UK is now working on a project to set up a diabetes prevention programme in a rural area of Guyana with the help of an eminent British specialist.

Beds for Guy
Peter Ramra
Deadl

Wandsworth Borough News – Beds to Guyana. (sitting, Dee McEvoy, Planning and Projects Manager at South West London and St. George's Mental Health Trust. Lower right employees from SOLK who transported the beds to Felixstowe (for free) prior to shipping to Guyana.

CHAPTER 16

HEALTH BUILDINGS FRAMEWORKS FOR THE FUTURE

SPREADING THE MESSAGE – Pro Cure 21/P21+

As mentioned on previous pages P21 and its successor P21+ are Department of Health initiated framework with the objective of expediting the procurement process for construction and refurbishment of NHS facilities. There is no compulsion to use framework but since the original P21 started in 2003 (and its successor P21+) over 600 schemes have been registered, collectively worth £3.5 billion. It is arguably one of the most successful government frameworks in the UK. One of its features was to promote leadership of schemes by experienced and qualified project staff.

The original concept of an NHS Accredited Project Director – Partnering by the Department of Health Estates Directorate - was that major capital projects (i.e those over £1million and up to £100 million) should ideally be managed by people who had completed the accreditation programme at Lancaster University. It was intended that graduates, on completion of a project would move from one Trust to another to spread good practice.

However, as sometimes happens with these centrally driven directives, they require the department or people promoting the initiative to be there and for commitment from operational hospital level. Subsequent organisational changes both at the Department of Health and within NHS Trusts meant that the original advice was lost. Every Trust made their own decision regarding the management and leadership of their major capital projects.

DEPARTMENT OF HEALTH

I had spent five and a half years managing two major mental health P21 projects, with a capital value of £30 million, which had been successfully completed. Another P21 project within the Trust or elsewhere in London or the South East was not immediately available. As an Accredited Project Director and graduate of the Lancaster University programme an opportunity to spread good practice at a national level arose. This came from being appointed in May 2009 as the Department of Health's P21 Implementation Adviser (IA) for the London and South East region. I joined a team of four IAs covering the rest of England. The five of us – Patrick Nolan, Terry Finch, Andy Mitchell and David Scamell formed an effective and productive team supporting Trusts across the country as they embarked on new projects. The fact that the five of us brought a variety of experience and skills helped us to be supportive of each other and enjoying each other's company was an added bonus.

In London and South East projects in this high profile area of the country had dried up. This was because of the absence of a locally based IA and also NHS Boards and their Estates professionals continued scepticisms of using nationally recommended frameworks. What was needed was someone with direct personal (and successful) experience of using the framework to stimulate interest and to break down barriers. I was given the task 'to provide expertise and guidance to Strategic Health Authorities, NHS Trusts and other NHS organisations undertaking clinical service reviews, reconfigurations and capital investments projects." Mentoring, mediating and providing up-to-date professional healthcare policy advice and support to clients were also included in the remit.

"Peter, Sahib, please explain a little more about NHS capital investment projects?"

"Basdeo, capital investment projects vary in size and complexity. From the upgrading of a hospital ward or a clinical department costing between £250,000 and £1million to the development of a new hospital at a cost of £100 million+. Developing business cases to support projects and piloting them through the various approval levels are expertise and skills which are sometimes not readily available within a hospital. In these cases outside consultancy advice is sought or the use of frameworks such as P21+ where advice is provided without cost by trained advisers."

"Thanks, Peter Sahib, please continue"

Word spread within London and South East and in the first six months I had signed up over 14 Trusts with individual capital values ranging from £10 million to £100 million. Within two years there was a substantial increase amounting to £325 million. The main contractors on the framework were overjoyed. The senior Programme Manager, Ray Stephenson and the Head of P21+ in Leeds, Pete Sellars were impressed. Was this just luck or were there other more complex issues at play? My view was that having a senior person who had successfully used the framework to give detailed presentations and respond authoritatively to questions (in particular from Trust Board members) allayed their fears. The potential for success in using the process was recognised and forward thinking Trusts took the plunge. The seeds which I had sown have blossomed. Currently (2015) several of the Trusts which had received presentations and/or embarked on the P21+ programme have continued with further projects, with one current scheme (2015) registered at £200 million.

Working across the region gave me a deeper understanding of the variations within the NHS and a greater appreciation of the issues that bind the NHS family. Everyone was battling with financial austerity, the constantly changing national agenda (some of which was felt not be fully thought through) and a recurring view that the NHS estate (one of the largest in Europe) was not given the appropriate focus and understanding which it deserves, particularly its potential for significant financial contribution (currently in 2015, estimated at £7.5billion) to emerging clinical strategies. With austerity measures continuing to bite and the Department of Health shedding fixed term Advisers, it was time to move on, returning once again to management consultancy.

***

GUYCON HEALTHCARE MANAGEMENT CONSULTANCY LIMITED

In 2003 I had registered a company, Guycon Healthcare Management Consultancy Limited, which laid dormant for eight years whilst working contractually with, firstly the NHS, then with the Department of Health. On leaving the department in 2011 there was general recognition that the success which I had achieved in significantly stimulating interest in, and sign up to, the P21/P21+ programme in London and South East would be lost if the service I had provided could not immediately continue albeit in a different format. Guycon was activated to provide freelance consultancy advice. Working with the healthcare directors of the six major construction firms on the framework – Kier (Gary Barnes), Balfour Beatty (Keith Hayes), Willmott Dixon (Michael Clarke), Interserve (Andrew Jowett) , Integrated Health Projects (Alan Kondys) and Miller HPS (Andy Cartwright) we agreed a marketing plan and a briefing document on P21 from the Principal Supply Chain Partners perspective. All the Directors were most helpful and supportive, Gary and Alan went the 'extra mile' to ensure that the new arrangements were effectively in place and the outcomes reflected the needs of the firms.

The change from being a DH employee to a freelance consultant (my new business card showing the logo of the six firms brought a wry smile from NHS colleagues!) went very smoothly. I continued the level of sign -ups (of P21+ projects) that I had enjoyed in my previous role. In two and half years, 23 major projects were registered with a capital value of £350 million. My reward and satisfaction were that around London and South East England I had contributed to the refurbishment or development of new capital investment facilities which would make a considerable difference to the well- being and comfort of patients.

As a freelance consultant I was also able to provide my services as Strategic Healthcare Advisor to Pick Everard, one of the leading, independent and multi- disciplinary architectural and engineering partnerships in the UK. Established in the 1860s, their head office was in Leicester but they also had offices throughout England and Scotland, including central London. They were referred to me by

P21+ headquarters as a firm seeking a conversation with someone who had expert knowledge of the NHS in general and P21+ in particular. The practice wanted to develop further in these areas. An initial and most pleasant meeting with one of their Partners, David Nesbit and a Director, Paul Rothera, both of whom already had a significant knowledge of the NHS, convinced me that associating with the Practice would be a mutually enriching experience. And so it turned out. For me it this was yet another opportunity to share my skills and experiences with people who were keen to make a difference to the built environment for patient care and who understood the public sector ethos. I was very impressed hearing of the award winning work which they had carried out in other sectors and felt that their experience and skills matched the needs of the health sector.

Department of Health, P21 Implementation Advisers. L to R back David Scammell, Terry Finch, Andy Mitchell, front Patrick Nolan, author.

CHAPTER 17

STRONGER ECONOMY, FAIRER SOCIETY
GETTING ON IN LIFE

POLITICAL ACTIVITIES – LIBERAL DEMOCRATS

Freed from employment contracts with the NHS and the Department of Health, I felt that I was now able to become more active with the Liberal Democrats. Although throughout the period I had taken a passionate interest in some of the burning issues of the day e.g. the financial crisis, race relations, immigration and the Middle East wars, I had done so as an activist of the Lib Dems but not as an officer holder of the Party. I had not being directly involved in the management of the Party at local level nor in the development of policy. In 2011 I was elected to the local Lewisham Executive and in June of that year I sent an email offering my services nationally to Norman Lamb, Liberal Democrat Member of Parliament and at the time Parliamentary Private Secretary to the Deputy Prime Minister, Nick Clegg. Almost immediately came the reply:

"Come and meet me at Portcullis House," the building near to the Houses of Parliament which provides office space for MPs and their staff. The speed of the response (normally you would have to wait weeks to meet a senior MP particularly if you were not in his or her constituency), the quality of the discussion and the advice given, spurred me on. Importantly, I got a feel for the areas in which it would be best for me to contribute my skills and experience. I wanted to contribute to policy discussions in the public sector in general and the health services in particular. Within a short space of time I was also elected to the Lib Dems London Region Executive and the English Council.

I was now learning and contributing to the Party's discussions on policy and management and issues at local, regional and national levels. These exposures gave me a solid understanding of the Party's machinery and enabled me to play a full part when issues at these lower levels were picked for final discussion (and possible agreement) at the twice yearly Autumn and Spring Conferences. The democratic nature of the party allowed for all members to attend these conferences, speak on issues which were being debated and vote if they were a Federal Conference representative (now being reviewed so that any member attending could vote). Attendance at these conferences also gave members networking opportunities to meet colleagues from across the country, our MPs and Ministers. Having photographs taken with them or other grandees of the Party, especially if you were a new conference attendee, served as a small memento and were sometimes used in local Party publicity material. I initially joined in the fun but after a few conferences I had acquired all the mementoes I needed!

My 40+ years' work in healthcare led me to be passionately concerned about Mental Health and Public Finance Initiative (PFI) used by hospital Trusts. I sought to use my experience to contribute to debate and influence Party's actions and decisions wherever possible and appropriate.

Having spent many years in Mental Health and Learning Disability Trusts, I recognised the need to put more resources into these areas and to strive for equality of treatment (termed 'parity of esteem') for mental health and physical conditions. I was also concerned about the disproportionate number of black people, mainly African and Afro Caribbean people, who were in-patients and in other of parts of mental services in England. I was always looking for an opportunity to highlight this serious concern and this came at the 2012 Autumn Conference in Brighton.

Our local Lewisham Party had discussed and put forward several amendments to policy papers covering Early Years; Getting the Most out of Schools; Good Food Shouldn't Cost the Earth and Addressing the Under- Provision in Mental Health. All were accepted for discussion at conference. Speaking as the proposer for the mental health amendments, I called attention to a document called 'Count me IN... census results 2010 which showed that 23% of mental health in-patients were from Black and Ethnic Minority (BME). The paper also suggested a new strategy to tackle the ways in which people from certain BME communities come in contact with mental health services to reduce racial inequalities and improve the level of services delivered to these communities. The amendments were overwhelmingly approved. In subsequent conferences and policy initiatives, the focus on mental health has continued.

The second major issue which I was seeking to contribute to was the Party's policy on and support for PFIs and in particular their current damaging effects on the finances of NHS Hospital Trusts.

PFI in summary is a type of mortgage whereby the private sector funds public sector projects (in the NHS major hospital projects) over a period of time (20-30 years) during which Trusts have to repay the debt at the agreed rate of interest. In the NHS it was meant to speed up the building of new hospitals, provide maintenance for the building for the duration of the contract and allow the debt to remain off the Trust's balance sheet.

Amongst the many economic problems left by the previous Labour Government, many Liberal Democrat members locally felt that PFI was the most toxic. We estimated that the total capital costs to the Department of Health was £11.6 billion and would cost individual NHS Hospital Trusts £80 billion in repayments over the periods of the contracts. We believed that this placed an enormous burden on the shoulders of Trusts and was having a harmful impact on providing patient care.

Our local Party wanted something to be done about this and at the Glasgow Conference 2013 I was the mover of a policy motion - 'Impact on the Private Finance Initiative on the National Health Service.' In my speech I called for all contactors who were locked into PFI deals to be identified and for the contractual arrangements entered into with NHS Trusts to be made public; for the naming and shaming of those who refused to respond and for new regulatory controls on existing PFI providers that ban the transfer of ownership of contracts and assets to offshore tax havens. The motion was overwhelmingly approved with much hand clapping. I was happy –

for patients on whose behalf we were asking for action to be taken; for my local party who had shared my concerns and, personally, as I had correctly reflected the mood of the party and, more generally, for those who care for the wellbeing of our fellow citizens.

As Liberal Democrats were in government, as part of the coalition with the Conservatives, I felt that our Ministers, Peers and MPs would look for opportunities to promote the key aspects, if not the full conference support, on Mental Health and PFI and in time they would make their way into government policy. Although in the scheme of things these were relatively minor issues, the process through which they travelled gave me enormous satisfaction in contributing to my country's democratic decision making and confirmation that being involved in politics could have positive outcomes.

As my general health management expertise, skills and political activities became more widely known, I was invited to join the Party's Public Sector Working Group to prepare a policy document – 'Protecting Public Services and Making Them Work for You'. Set up by the Federal Policy Committee (FPC- one of the top decision making groups in the Party) The group's remit was to prepare a policy paper which would go to the FPC for approval prior to its presentation to the wider Party at one of the annual conferences. Approval there would lead to its recommendations being considered for inclusion in the Party's 2015 manifesto. Should our Party be in government after the elections, the expectation would be that some of the recommendations would become government policy.

The Working Party consisted of 21 members of the Party. There were Peers, MPs, ex MPs, Councillors, technical experts and ordinary members. From August 2013, for nearly 8 months, most of us met every other week (other than the Chair I was able to attend all but two!). In the last few months, this changed to once a week to discuss our approaches to schools, health and transport. We were informed by receiving a wide range of policy papers and also evidence in-person from a variety of senior experts in the three areas, including our own Lib Dem Ministers and a former Minister. This was an absolutely fascinating exercise in the development of policy. By April 2014 we had put the paper together, ironed out differences of emphasis and or/opinions, and it was ready to go to FPC and Conference for approval. I and no doubt my other colleagues were pleased when at 2014 Autumn Conference in Glasgow our paper was overwhelmingly approved. We now wait to see which parts of it will appear in the 2015 manifesto!

Activities on the Working Party also coincided with 2014 London Borough Council elections; the European Parliament Elections and for Lewisham Borough elections for Mayor. As Vice Chair of the Local Lewisham Party I had to be involved in all three.

For the council elections I was selected to stand for Blackheath ward (where I live); for the European Parliament we needed to support our sitting Member, Baroness Sarah Ludford and for the Mayoral elections we had a strong candidate in Councillor Duwayne Brooks who had a national profile as he was with his friend Stephen Lawrence, a teenager who was murdered in a racial incident in 1999.Considerable press coverage followed the incident. The failure of police to properly investigate the murder led to the Macpherson Inquiry which concluded that the Metropolitan Police was institutionally racist, but found no evidence of corruption. Over the years intermittent media commentary and analysis of the aftermath of the incident kept the names of those involved, including Duwayne in the public's mind.

Faced with three elections we had to concentrate our resources to bring about the best results. Blackheath was one of the target wards in the constituency. We had as one of the three sitting councillors for the ward Chris Maines, who was also the leader of the 10 Liberal Democrats group on Lewisham Borough Council. As there were 3 councillor places in the ward to be filled, Chris and I were joined by Adam Nathan who like both of us was a Blackheath resident and campaigner.

My last campaign for a council seat was in 1986 and here I was 28 years later trying again. In 1986 as Social Democrat/Alliance candidate for St. Mildred's ward in another part of the Borough (where I lived at the time) the campaign was relatively low key. We were new on the political scene, not in government and did not have to defend actions taken at a national level. Now, we were in government and, although we had delivered on 75% of our manifesto's commitments and worked 'to build a stronger economy in a fairer society enabling everyone to get on in life', we knew that we would be punished for the perceived wrongs of the government at national level. What we didn't fully appreciate was the extent of that punishment.

I threw myself into the campaigns – door knocking, telephone canvassing, raising petitions and delivering thousands of leaflets. I gained tremendous knowledge of the local electorate, found streets that I didn't know existed and saw the variety of accommodation within Blackheath ward- from the million pounds houses surrounding the heath to the multi storey council flats. Many of these flats had no lift and others had such tiny lifts that I was wary of using them – I opted to use the stairs. I was left wondering how people managed to get their weekly shopping or other heavy loads to their homes. Most people I encountered were pleasant, some engaged with me for long periods, giving detailed account of all their concerns and promising they would give me their vote if I kept my word. Not wishing to mislead I would explain what was possible and what was not, in the hope that honesty would result in a tick on the right place of the voting card.

For the Mayoral campaign we had a local boost when the Deputy Prime Minister (DPM) and leader of our Party, Nick Clegg, agreed to attend a fundraising dinner at a local hotel. The feeling was that this high profile visit would not only acknowledge the leadership support for our candidate but would spur on our members to become more involved. And yes, there was the need to raise cash.

A small group from the Campaign Committee was set up to arrange the visit internally. I was given the task of developing the formal proposal for the visit and for liaising with the DPM's office regarding the details of the evening including security. In the NHS as a Director I had experience of arranging ministerial and other VIP visits, but not for someone so much in the public eye and as senior as the DPM. Security concerns were of course very important, as was the need to ensure that they did not impede the contact with attendees. Everything went smoothly and we were pleased that adequate funds were raised and everyone had a good time.

We needed to ensure that our local campaign integrated with the Mayoral and European elections and we did our utmost to achieve this. Sarah Ludford was an energetic campaigner, who visited us on several occasions. She door knocked, delivered leaflets and posed for the obligatory photographs for local activists (for Blackheath, with Chris, Adam and I in Greenwich Park with Canary Wharf in the background!) We were all impressed by her experience, her vast knowledge of European Parliament issues and her warmth.

Regrettably, despite the extensive work put into our four target seats, the substantial promises and indication of support for the Mayoral campaign and an excellent MEP candidate, we lost in all three areas. Significantly we lost all ten of our council seats.

Our feeling was that although we had good responses at the doorstep, many of our supporters had either not voted or on this occasion gave the other Parties the benefit of the doubt. We also felt that local achievements and issues were overtaken by national concerns. As part of the Government we had to accept responsibility for the electorates' views of our performance and learn the lessons from the Coalition we had formed.

We now had to refocus and rebuild.

"Peter Sahib, you have given a very condensed view of some significant recent activities. Was this intentional, are you saving more information for another book at a later time?"

"Yes Basdeo, it was intentionally a summary of activities. To go in detail would be too much for the reader, after a canter through nearly six decades of activities. But my commitment to the Party has continued and in 2014 I was elected as Secretary to the London Region Executive and Chair of the Lewisham Party for 2015. Not too sure about another book, but only time will tell!

***

70th Birthday

During my consultancies and political activities I reached the biblical three score and ten on 10th October, 2013! As mentioned in previous pages the extended family constantly kept in touch and my sister Ena, niece Vimla Kishna and nephew Peter Ronald Ramsaroop thought it would be a good idea if we could all get together in Guyana and visit some of the places I had, over the years, discussed with them and see what progress had been made. This turned out to be a fascinating experience which touched me deeply as I not only enjoyed travelling down 'memory lane' but it was all funded as my unique early birthday treat! As I was in Guyana during the Queen's birthday celebrations (June 2013) I was invited to the British High Commission's to mark the event. In a most enjoyable and relaxed environment I was able to meet the President, Prime Minister, Foreign Minister and a wide range of leaders and shakers to share and compare developments (particularly during the past 50 years) in the UK and Guyana - as a UK citizen I felt really recycled! A subsequent visit to Baganara Island, one of Guyana's finest eco- resorts on the Essequibo River, and what I had seen during my travels, confirmed to me that, in certain areas, the country had made substantial progress for which all Guyanese should be justifiably proud.

Back in the UK for my actual birthday a pre-arranged visit (kept as a surprise) to the Royal Air Force museum in Hendon, north London and a celebratory dinner were extremely thoughtful and much appreciated gestures which topped up a period of reminisces.

Peter Ramrayka lives in Morden Hill.

Peter has lived in Blackheath for nearly 10 years and has been very involved in local health issues. A member of Lewisham and Greenwich NHS Trust and elected to the Lewisham Health and Wellbeing Board, Peter has been fighting to keep services at Lewisham Hospital. He Chairs voluntary organisations involved with community relations and with healthcare projects abroad.

Peter is concerned at the Council's poor record of consulting on planning issues. He feels they have failed to keep residents informed about the Lewisham town centre, despite the disruptive impact it will have on our area.

Conservatives know there is only one way to beat Labour in Blackheath

Local elections in Blackheath and Lewisham are between the Liberal Democrats and Labour. The Conservatives are weak locally unable to field candidates everywhere and struggling to have a presence on the Council. The opposition in Lewisham has been provided by the Liberal Democrats. – holding Labour's Mayor to account – exposing failing services and wasted spending.

22nd May – Vote for Three

Only the Lib Dems or Labour can win here

| Can't Win | Lab 30% | Lib Dem 33% |

BLACKHEATH'S LOCAL CHOICE

people who live here and care about our area

Councillors

Chris Maines lives in Brandram Road. He works hard with local residents to protect Blackheath, succeeding in it being awarded Green Flag status for the last 3 years. He is keen to balance the different uses of the heath and has ensured residents are better informed about large events and road closures. Chris has Chaired Blackheath Assembly for the last 4 years – getting funds spent on local facilities particularly for young people and the elderly.

Adam Nathan lives in Lee Park. He supports the London Cycling Campaign to make Blackheath village a more cycle and pedestrian friendly area. Lewisham Council have turned down grants to help make cycling in the Borough safer. Adam has been talking to companies about opening a cinema in Lewisham town centre. Lewisham is one of the few London boroughs without any cinema.

Peter Ramrayka lives in Morden Hill. He is campaigning to get South Eastern Railway to reopen the platform 4 gates at Lewisham Station, particularly during the town centre redevelopment. Peter has been involved with the fight to keep services at Lewisham Hospital. He has been elected by the voluntary groups in the borough to represent them on the new Health and Wellbeing board.

Mayor of Lewisham

Duwayne Brooks lives in Deptford, and has grown up in Lewisham. His history and background give him a unique insight into the borough and it's problems, which means he can provide a vision for Lewisham that is unique and refreshing. Duwayne is campaigning for early intervention in schools, to prevent children from turning to crime. He plans to create new opportunities for businesses, and wants to put a stop to the endless stream of take away leaflets coming through your door.

MEP

The **Liberal Democrats** are standing up to protect the 3 Million jobs that depend on the European Union. Liberal Democrat MEP for London, **Sarah Ludford**, is fighting hard to keep Britain in the EU, and to ensure that Britain gets the best out of the EU. She has ensured that Britain keeps the European Arrest Warrant, which brings criminals to justice, even if they flee to other EU countries. Sarah also fights hard on environmental issues, which can only be solved by working together with our European neighbours.

Adam, Peter and Chris with Sarah Ludford, MEP for London

Liberal Democrats Blackheath Council candidates, Mayoral and European Elections flyer – May 2014.

Campaigning – with car to supplement tired legs.

Manning a stall to raise money for political activities.

With the Lord Mayor of London. Mansion House reception - 2014.

Campaigning for Victory for Lewisham Hospital, and we won!!

Simon Hughes, MP for Bermondsey and Old Southwark and Minister of State –
Ministry of Justice and some members of Lib Dems Ethnic Minority Group - 2015.

With Guyana's Prime Minister Sam Hinds, and Peter Ramsaroop – June 2013.

With Guyana's Opposition Leader - David Granger – June 2013.

70th Birthday treat – Royal Air Force Museum - October 2013.

70th Birthday drink! – October 2013.

Celebratory family gathering in Guyana with Ena and her children. L to R Peter, Vimla, Ena, author, Paul, Pamela and Robert - June 2013.

Enjoying Guyanese cuisine at Baganara Eco resort – June 2013 (from left Vimla, her husband Aubrey, Ena and author).

Supporting UN Anti- Racism Day 2015 with colleagues from Liberal Democrats Ethnic minority group, Simon Hughes, MP and Lynne Featherstone,MP, Minister of State at the Home Office.

Nick Clegg – Deputy Prime Minster - at Lib Dems Annual Conference.

With John and Ena – Bedford – England – 2013.

EPILOGUE

In the preceding pages, with my travelling companion a Bacoo named Basdeo, I have recounted my memories from my early days in what was then British Guiana to the present time. The narrative deliberately concentrated on the working and professional aspects of my life including those who have interacted with me at work as I sought to make a difference in health, voluntary work and politics.

In highlighting the transition of my family's history from Indian indentured labourers to becoming part of the middle classes in a developing colonial society, I have given a glimpse of the challenges which were overcome. Moving from a relatively comfortable environment in British Guiana and growing up in one of the most advanced and fair societies in the world, yet tarnished with broad streaks of racial prejudice (colour and culture being dominating factors) required understanding, patience and resilience.

The last 50 years have seen remarkable changes in British society. The considerable improvements in healthcare and the health and wellbeing of citizens have been briefly mentioned but are fully documented in other specialists' books. Information technology and communications have also had a considerable impact on our work and social life with nearly everyone having access to computers and mobile phones. New laws have to a certain extent kept up with changing views of society and within a relatively short period of time we have had the decriminalisation of homosexuality, the introduction of the Abortion Act 1967 (making it legal to abort a pregnancy, under certain conditions, if it had not exceeded twenty four weeks), the Equal Pay Acts - equal pay for men and women doing similar jobs - and the approval of the Anglican Church to ordain female bishops. Race relations in Britain are moving in a similar more liberal direction but have to contend with centuries old deep rooted prejudices, some of them based on mis-information, fear and notions of racial supremacy. It is for the coming generation schooled and growing up together to break down these barriers and in large metropolitan cities there is ample evidence that this is being achieved.

In the wider world there was growth of religious fundamentalism fuelled by perceived wrongs and exacerbated by controversial wars in Iraq, Afghanistan and elsewhere which many saw as not achieving their set objectives.

We live in a period of apprehension. To some people the crop of recent and current world leaders do not inspire confidence as they are seen not to have the depth of understanding, life experiences or leadership skills which their high positions demand. Many appear to get by on advice which on many occasions has been found to be inaccurate.

At my humble level my mission is to continue to share my knowledge, skills and experience in areas which give me the greatest satisfaction – professional health management consultancies, political activities with the Liberal Democrats, voluntary services (particularly overseas) and with the Royal Air Forces Association to continue to support the RAF Family. As Chairman of the City and Central London Branch I participated (for the first time) in Remembrance Sunday in 2014, marching after 40 years (as part of the Federation of the Old Comrades Association) from the service at St. Paul's Cathedral to the London Troops Memorial at the Royal Exchange in the City for the Wreath Laying Ceremony was a reminder of my RAF service. As we were given the command "eye left" (whilst marching straight) to salute the Lord Mayor, memories of my square bashing days in the RAF floated back and I had goose pimples. After the formalities a most refreshing luncheon at Mansion House compensated for tired legs.

I was also pleased to be elected as one of the community representatives on the Health and Wellbeing Board of Lewisham Borough Council, a new health and social care organisation charged with bringing together at a local level the National Health Service, public health, adult social care and children services, to plan how best to meet the needs of the local population and tackle inequalities in health. A tall order but where there is a will there is a way! I have in mind the Royal Air Force's motto:

Per Ardua Ad Astra – 'Through Adversity to the Stars."